VERSIONS
OF
ACADEMIC
FREEDOM

Versions *of* Academic Freedom

FROM PROFESSIONALISM TO REVOLUTION

Stanley Fish

THE
UNIVERSITY
OF CHICAGO
PRESS
*Chicago and
London*

STANLEY FISH is
the Davidson-Kahn
Distinguished
University Professor
and Professor of
Law at Florida
International
University and
the Floersheimer
Distinguished
Visiting Professor of
Law at Benjamin N.
Cardozo School of
Law.

The University of Chicago Press, Chicago 60637

The University of Chicago Press, Ltd., London

© 2014 by Stanley Fish

All rights reserved. Published 2014.

Printed in the United States of America

23 22 21 20 19 18 17 16 15 14 1 2 3 4 5

ISBN-13: 978-0-226-06431-4 (cloth)

ISBN-13: 978-0-226-17025-1 (e-book)

DOI: 10.7208/chicago/9780226170251.001.0001

Library of Congress Cataloging-in-Publication Data

Fish, Stanley Eugene, author.

   Versions of academic freedom : from

professionalism to revolution / Stanley Fish.

      pages cm. — (Rice University Campbell

lectures)

   Includes bibliographical references and index.

      ISBN 978-0-226-06431-4 (cloth : alk. paper) —

ISBN 978-0-226-17025-1 (e-book) 1. Freedom of

speech — United States. 2. Academic freedom —

United States. 3. Intellectual freedom — United

States. 4. United States. Constitution 1st

Amendment. 5. Civil service — United States. I. Title.

   KF4772.F5677 2014

   371.1′04 — dc23

                                          2014013079

To

WILLIAM VAN ALSTYNE,

colleague and friend

CONTENTS

PREFACE

This is a thesis book, which means that it does not pretend to be a comprehensive treatment of its subject. The list of the topics it slights is at least as long as the list of the topics it includes. I attempt to survey the quite large literature about academic freedom and to distill from it a taxonomy of approaches. That taxonomy is at once philosophical and political, and only occasionally historical and empirical. I am interested in the ways people talk about academic freedom and in the presuppositions (about truth, the purpose of education, and the social/political function of the academy) implied by their talk. This interest leads me in some directions and away from others. I do not, for example, say much about tenure, unionization, the rise of contingent faculty, the decline in the funding of state universities, the rewards and perils of partnerships with industry, the impact of technology, the changes in the world of publishing, the culture wars, terrorism, or globalism. Each of these has a relationship to academic freedom that deserves, and has often received, extended attention. But not here.

Nor do I take into account the shape of academic freedom in countries other than the United States. Some of the needed comparative work has been ably done by Eric Barendt (2010) in his *Academic Freedom and the Law: A Comparative Study.* Barendt observes that in some ways academic freedom in the United States "is a much more complex subject than it is in the United Kingdom or Germany, where the freedom is based respectively on a statutory right (the UK Education Reform Act, 1988) or a constitutional right (the German Basic Law)" (162). Much of the discussion of academic freedom in this country is generated by the absence of any such clear foundation for its claims—in contrast, say, to New Zealand, where the Education Act of 1989 provides authoritative answers to questions that are untethered to any authority in the US: What is the purpose of academic freedom? Who has it? What relation does it have to "public accountability"? These and related questions are raised all the time in both legal and academic contexts in America, but as J. Peter Byrne (1989) has memorably said, "lacking definition or guiding principle, the doctrine [of academic freedom] floats in the law, picking up decisions as a hull does barnacles" (251).

The matter is complicated by the fact that there are (at least) two distinct concepts of academic freedom: one legal, the other professional. The professional concept of academic freedom is the product of the guild's desire (shared with other guilds) to order its own affairs with a minimum of interference from the outside; academic freedom is the freedom, first, to pursue professional goals, and, second, to specify for itself the appropriate means of realizing those goals. The profession is jealous of its prerogatives and reluctant to yield them to other authorities, including the authority of the courts.

The legal concept of academic freedom (to the extent that there is one) centers on the relationship between guild desires and legal obligations. Is the freedom academics claim compatible with generally applicable laws in the areas where the freedom is being asserted? Or, to put the question another way, does academic freedom have a significant legal identity? This question is much debated in the literature, and I agree with those who say that while courts occasionally invoke the doctrine, the decisions that follow are typically reached on other, more traditional grounds, such as tax law, contract law, public employee law, etc.. Academic freedom is rhetorically strong but legally weak. Indeed, it is not at all clear that academic freedom has any substantial presence in the law. Rather than being homologous or even overlapping, the professional and legal concepts of academic freedom seem to be disconnected.

Some scholars labor to bring the professional and legal concepts of academic freedom into line, either by asserting that academic freedom is essential to democratic government, or by conflating academic freedom with the right of free expression. I find these efforts unpersuasive for reasons to be given later. In what follows, academic freedom will be characterized as a professional project that claims, but never quite achieves, legal and constitutional status. The claim of legal status depends on the prior claim that academics are special, even exceptional, and, because exceptional, exempt from the rules and regulations that apply to others. This thesis—I call it academic exceptionalism—has been put forward in the courts, but, more often than not, it has been rejected. (I tell this story in chapter 5.) But if the claim of exceptionalism is rejected, what remains of academic freedom; that is, of a freedom peculiarly granted to academics? If academics are really just like anyone else, on what basis, if any, can academic freedom be justified? Justification is always the challenge academic freedom must meet, and it is with the issue of justification that we shall begin.

ACKNOWLEDGMENTS

I want to first acknowledge Rice University and Dean Nicolas Shumway for inviting me to give the Campbell Lectures in 2012 and I want to thank Cary Wolfe for his many good offices. I am grateful to an embarassingly large number of friends and colleagues who took the time to read the manuscript and comment on it: Larry Alexander, Judith Areen, Hanoch Dagan, Peter Goodrich, Gerald Graff, Gary Olson, Michael Robertson, Fred Schauer, Martin Stone, William Van Alstyne, and Ernest Weinrib. And finally I am indebted to Alan Thomas, Anita Samen, and Yvonne Zipter of the University of Chicago Press. None of this would have been possible without the invaluable aid of my research assistants, Lian de la Riva and Stephanie Dimitrakis.

1

ACADEMIC FREEDOM STUDIES
The Five Schools

In 2009 Terrence Karran published an essay with the title "Academic Freedom: In Justification of a Universal Ideal." Although it may not seem so at first glance, the title is tendentious, for it answers in advance the question most often posed in the literature: How does one justify academic freedom? One justifies academic freedom, we are told before Karran's analysis even begins, by claiming for it the status of a universal ideal.

The advantage of this claim is that it disposes of one of the most frequently voiced objections to academic freedom: Why should members of a particular profession be granted latitudes and exemptions not enjoyed by other citizens? Why, for example, should college and university professors be free to criticize their superiors when employees in other workplaces might face discipline or dismissal? Why should college and university professors be free to determine and design the condition of their workplace (the classroom) while others must adhere to a blueprint laid down by a supervisor? Why should college and university professors be free to choose the direction of their research while researchers who work for industry and government must go down the paths mandated by their employers? We must ask, says Frederick Schauer (2006), "whether academics should, by virtue of their academic employment and/or profession, have rights (or privileges, to be more accurate) not possessed by others" (913).

The architects of the doctrine of academic freedom were not unaware of these questions, and, in anticipation of others raising them, raised them themselves. Academic freedom, wrote Arthur O. Lovejoy (1930), might seem "peculiar chiefly in that the teacher is . . . a salaried employee and that the freedom claimed for him implies a denial of the right of those who provide or administer the funds from which he is paid to control the content of his teaching" (384). But this denial of the employer's control of the employee's behavior is peculiar only if one assumes, first, that college and university teaching is a job like any other and, second, that the college or university teacher works for a dean or a provost or a board of trustees. Those assumptions are directly challenged and rejected by the American Association of University Professors' 1915 Declaration of Principles on Academic Freedom and Academic Tenure, a founding document (of which Lovejoy was a principal author) and one that is, in many respects, still authoritative. Here is a key sentence:

> The responsibility of the university teacher is primarily to the public itself, and to the judgment of his own profession; and while, with respect to certain external conditions of his vocation, he accepts a responsibility to the authorities of the institution in which he serves, in the essentials of his professional activity his duty is to the wider public to which the institution itself is morally amenable.

There are four actors and four centers of interest in this sentence: the public, the institution of the academy, the individual faculty member, and the individual college or university. The faculty member's allegiance is first to the public, an abstract entity that is not limited to a particular location. The faculty member's secondary allegiance is to the judgment of his own profession, but since, as the text observes, the profession's responsibility is to the public, it amounts to the same thing. Last in line is the actual college or university to which the faculty member is tied by the slightest of ligatures. He must honor the "external conditions of his vocation"—conditions like showing up in class and assigning grades, and holding office hours and teaching to the syllabus and course catalog (although, as we shall see, those conditions are not always considered binding)—but since it is a "vocation" to which the faculty member is responsible, he will always have his eye on what is really essential, the "universal ideal" that underwrites and justifies his labors.

Here in 1915 are the seeds of everything that will flower in the twenty-first century. The key is the distinction between a job and a vocation. A job is defined by an agreement (often contractual) between a worker and a boss: you will do X and I will pay you Y; and if you fail to perform as stipulated, I will discipline or even dismiss you. Those called to a vocation are not merely workers; they are professionals; that is, they profess something larger than the task immediately at hand—a religious faith, a commitment to the rule of law, a dedication to healing, a zeal for truth—and in order to become credentialed professors, as opposed to being amateurs, they must undergo a rigorous and lengthy period of training. Being a professional is less a matter of specific performance (although specific performances are required) than of a continual, indeed lifelong, responsiveness to an ideal or a spirit. And given that a spirit, by definition, cannot be circumscribed, it will always be possible (and even thought mandatory and laudable) to expand the area over which it is said to preside.

The history of academic freedom is in part the history of that expansion as academic freedom is declared to be indistinguishable from, and necessary for, the flourishing of every positive value known to humankind. Here are just a few quotations from Karran's essay:

> Academic freedom is important to everyone's well-being, as well as being particularly pertinent to academics and their students. (The Robbins Committee on Higher Education in the UK, 1963)

Academic freedom is but a facet of freedom in the larger society. (R. M. O. Pritchard, "Academic Freedom and Autonomy in the United Kingdom and Germany," 1998)

A democratic society is hardly conceivable . . . without academic freedom. (S. Bergan, "Institutional Autonomy: Between Myth and Responsibility," 2002)

In a society that has a high regard for knowledge and universal values, the scope of academic freedom is wide. (Wan Manan, "Academic Freedom: Ethical Implications and Civic Responsibilities," 2000)

The sacred trust of the universities is to carry the torch of freedom. (J. W. Boyer, "Academic Freedom and the Modern University: The Experience of the University of Chicago," 2002)

Notice that in this last statement, *freedom* is not qualified by the adjective *academic*. Indeed, you can take it as a rule that the larger the claims for academic freedom, the less the limiting force of the adjective *academic* will be felt. In the taxonomy I offer in this book, the movement from the most conservative to the most radical view of academic freedom will be marked by the transfer of emphasis from *academic*, which names a local and specific habitation of the asserted freedom, to *freedom*, which does not limit the scope or location of what is being asserted at all.

Of course, freedom is itself a contested concept and has many possible meanings. Graeme C. Moodie sorts some of them out and defines the freedom academics might reasonably enjoy in terms more modest than those suggested by the authors cited in Karran's essay. Moodie (1996) notes that freedom is often understood as the "absence of constraint," but that, he argues, would be too broad an understanding if it were applied to the activities of academics. Instead he would limit academic freedom to faculty members who are "exercising academic functions in a truly academic matter" (134). Academic freedom, in his account, follows from the nature of academic work; it is not a personal right of those who choose to do that work. That freedom—he calls it an "activity freedom" because it flows from the nature of the job and not from some moral abstraction—"can of course only be exercised by persons, but its justification, and thus its extent, must clearly and explicitly be rooted in its relationship to academic activities rather than (or only consequentially) to the persons who perform them" (133). In short, he concludes, "the special freedom(s) of academics is/are conditional on the fulfillment of their academic obligations" (134).

Unlike those who speak of a universal ideal and of the torch of freedom being carried everywhere, Moodie is focused on the adjective *academic*. He begins with it and reasons from it to the boundaries of the freedom academics can legitimately be granted. To be sure, the matter is not so cut and dried, for *academic* must itself be defined so that those boundaries can come clearly into view and that is no easy matter. No one doubts that classroom teaching and research and scholarly publishing are activities where the freedom in question is to be accorded, at least to some extent. But what about the freedom to criticize one's superiors; or the freedom to configure a course in ways not standard in the department; or the freedom to have a voice in the building of parking garages, or in the funding of athletic programs, or in the decision to erect a student center, or in the selection of a president, or in the awarding of honorary degrees, or in the inviting of outside speakers? Is academic freedom violated when faculty members have minimal input into, or are shut out entirely from, the consideration of these and other matters?

To that question, Mark Yudof, who has been a law school dean and a university president, answers a firm "no." Yudof (1988) acknowledges that "there are many elements necessary to sustain the university," including "salaries," library collections," a "comfortable workplace," and even "a parking space" (1356), but do academics have a right to these things or a right to participate in discussions about them (a question apart from the question of whether it is wise for an administration to bring them in)? Only, says Yudof, if you believe "that any restrictions, however indirectly linked to teaching and scholarship, will destroy the quest for knowledge" (1355). And that, he observes, would amount to "a kind of unbridled libertarianism for academicians," who could say anything they liked in a university setting without fear of reprisal or discipline (1356).

Better, Yudof concludes, to define academic freedom narrowly, if only so those who are called upon to defend it can offer a targeted, and not wholly diffuse, rationale. Academic freedom, he declares, "is what it is" (of course that's the question; what is it?), and it is "not general liberty, pleasant working conditions, equality, self-realization, or happiness," for "if academic freedom is thought to include all that is desirable for academicians, it may come to mean quite little to policy makers and courts" (1356). Moodie (1996) gives an even more pointed warning: "Scholars only invite ridicule, or being ignored, when they seem to suggest that every issue that directly affects them is a proper sphere for academic rule" (146). (We shall revisit this issue when we consider the relationship between academic freedom, shared governance, and public employee law.)

So we now have as a working hypothesis an opposition between two views of academic freedom. In one, freedom is a general, overriding, and ever-expanding value, and the academy is just one of the places that house it. In the other, the freedom in question is peculiar to the academic profession and limited to the performance of its core duties. When performing those duties, the instructor is, at least relatively, free. When engaged in other activities, even those that take place within university precincts, no such freedom or special latitude obtains. This modest notion of academic freedom is strongly articulated by J. Peter Byrne (1989): "The term 'academic freedom' should be reserved for those rights necessary for the preservation of the unique functions of the university" (262).

These opposed accounts of academic freedom do not exhaust the possibilities; there are extremes to either side of them, and in the pages that follow I shall present the full range of the positions currently available. In effect I am announcing the inauguration of a new field—Academic Freedom Studies. The field is still in a fluid state; new variants and new theories continue to appear. But for the time being we can identify five schools of academic freedom, plotted on a continuum that goes from right to left. The continuum is obviously a political one, but the politics are the politics of the academy. Any correlation of the points on the continuum with real world politics is imperfect, but, as we shall see, there is some. I should acknowledge at the outset that I shall present these schools as more distinct than they are in practice; individual academics can be members of more than one of them. The taxonomy I shall offer is intended as a device of clarification. The inevitable blurring of the lines comes later.

As an aid to the project of sorting out the five schools, here is a list of questions that would receive different answers depending on which version of academic freedom is in place:

Is academic freedom a constitutional right?

What is the relationship between academic freedom and the First Amendment?

What is the relationship between academic freedom and democracy?

Does academic freedom, whatever its scope, attach to the individual faculty member or to the institution?

Do students have academic freedom rights?

What is the relationship between academic freedom and the form of governance at a college or university?

In what sense, if any, are academics special?

Does academic freedom include the right of a professor to criticize his or her organizational superiors with impunity?

Does academic freedom allow a professor to rehearse his or her political views in the classroom?

What is the relationship between academic freedom and political freedom?

What views of education underlie the various positions on academic freedom?

As a further aid, it would be good to have in mind some examples of incidents or controversies in which academic freedom has been thought to be at stake.

In 2011, the faculty of John Jay College nominated playwright Tony Kushner to be the recipient of an honorary degree from the City University of New York. Normally approval of the nomination would have been pro forma, but this time the CUNY Board of Trustees tabled, and thus effectively killed, the motion supporting Kushner's candidacy because a single trustee objected to his views on Israel. After a few days of outrage and bad publicity the board met again and changed its mind. Was the board's initial action a violation of academic freedom, and if so, whose freedom was being violated? Or was the incident just one more instance of garden-variety political jockeying, a tempest in a teapot devoid of larger implications?

In the same year Professor John Michael Bailey of Northwestern University permitted a couple to perform a live sex act at an optional session of his course on human sexuality. The male of the couple brought his naked female partner to orgasm with the help of a device known as a "fucksaw." Should Bailey have been reprimanded and perhaps disciplined for allowing lewd behavior in his classroom or should the display be regarded as a legitimate pedagogical choice and therefore protected by the doctrine of academic freedom?

In 2009 sociology professor William Robinson of the University of California at Santa Barbara, after listening to a tape of a Martin Luther King speech protesting the Vietnam War, sent an e-mail to the students in his sociology of globalization course that began:

> If Martin Luther King were alive on this day of January
> 19th, there is no doubt that he would be condemning
> the Israeli aggression against Gaza along with U.S.
> military and political support for Israeli war crimes, or
> that he would be standing shoulder to shoulder with the
> Palestinians.

The e-mail went on to compare the Israeli actions against Gaza to the Nazi actions against the Warsaw ghetto, and to characterize Israel as "a state founded on the negation of a people." Was Robinson's e-mail an intrusion of his political views into the classroom or was it a contribution to the subject matter of his course and therefore protected under the doctrine of academic freedom?

As the 2008 election approached, an official communication from the administration of the University of Illinois listed as prohibited political activities the wearing of T-shirts or buttons supporting candidates or parties. Were faculty members being denied their First Amendment and academic freedom rights?

BB&T, a bank holding company, funds instruction in ethics on the condition that the courses it supports include as a required reading Ayn Rand's *Atlas Shrugged* (certainly a book concerned with issues of ethics). If a university accepts this arrangement (as Florida State University did), has it traded its academic freedom for cash or is it (as the dean at Florida State insisted) merely accepting help in a time of financial exigency?

In 1996, the state of Virginia passed a law forbidding state employees from accessing pornographic materials on state-owned computers. The statute included a waiver for those who could convince a supervisor that the viewing of pornographic material was part of a bona fide research project. Was the academic freedom of faculty members in the state university system violated because they were prevented from determining for themselves and without government monitoring the course of their research?

Just as my questions would be answered differently by proponents of different accounts of academic freedom, so would these cases be assessed differently depending on which school of academic freedom a commentator belongs to.

Of course I have yet to name the schools, and I will do that now.

(1)— *The "It's just a job" school*. This school (which may have only one member and you're reading him now) rests on a deflationary view of higher education. Rather than being a vocation or holy calling, higher education is a service that offers knowledge and skills to students who wish to receive them. Those who work in higher education are trained to impart that knowledge, demonstrate those skills and engage in research that adds to the body of what is known. They are not exercising First Amendment rights or forming citizens or inculcating moral values or training soldiers to fight for social justice. Their obligations and aspirations are defined by the distinctive task—the advancement of knowledge—they are trained and paid to perform, defined, that is, by contract and by the course catalog rather than by a vision of democracy or world peace. College and university teachers are professionals, and as such the activities they legitimately perform are professional activities, activities in which they have a professional competence. When engaged in those activities, they should be accorded the latitude—call it freedom if you like—necessary to their proper performance. That latitude does not include the performance of other tasks, no matter how worthy they might be. According to this school, academics are not free in any special sense to do anything but their jobs.

(2)—*The "For the common good" school.* This school has its origin in the AAUP Declaration of Principles (1915), and it shares some arguments with the "It's just a job" school, especially the argument that the academic task is distinctive. Other tasks may be responsible to market or political forces or to public opinion, but the task of advancing knowledge involves following the evidence wherever it leads, and therefore "the first condition of progress is complete and unlimited freedom to pursue inquiry and publish its results." The standards an academic must honor are the standards of the academic profession; the freedom he enjoys depends on adherence to those standards: "The liberty of the scholar . . . to set forth his conclusions . . . is conditioned by their being conclusions being gained by a scholar's method and held in a scholar's spirit." That liberty cannot be "used as a shelter . . . for uncritical and intemperate partisanship," and a teacher should not inundate students with his "own opinions."

With respect to pronouncements like these, the "For the common good" school and the "It's just a job" school seem perfectly aligned. Both paint a picture of a self-enclosed professional activity, a transaction between teachers, students, and a set of intellectual questions with no reference to larger moral, political, or societal considerations. But the opening to larger considerations is provided, at least potentially, by a claimed connection between academic freedom and democracy. Democracy, say the authors of the 1915 Declaration, requires "experts . . . to advise both legislators and administrators," and it is the universities that will supply them and thus render a "service to the right solution of . . . social problems." Democracy's virtues, the authors of the Declaration explain, are also the source of its dangers, for by repudiating despotism and political tyranny, democracy risks legitimizing "the tyranny of public opinion." The academy rides to the rescue by working "to help make public opinion more self-critical and more circumspect, to check the more hasty and unconsidered impulses of popular feeling, to train the democracy." By thus offering an external justification for an independent academy—it protects us from our worst instincts and furthers the realization of democratic principles—the "For the common good" school moves away from the severe professionalism of the "It's just a job" school and toward an argument in which professional values are subordinated to the higher values of democracy or justice or freedom; that is, to the common good.

(3)—*The "Academic exceptionalism or uncommon beings" school.* This school is a logical extension of the "For the common good" school. If academics are charged not merely with the task of adding to our knowledge of natural and cultural phenomena, but with the task of providing a counterweight to the force of common popular opinion, they must themselves be *un*common, not only intellectually but morally; they must be, in the words of the 1915 Declaration, "men of high gift and character." Such men (and now women) not only correct the errors of popular opinion, they escape popular judgment and are not to be held accountable to the same laws and restrictions that constrain ordinary citizens.

The essence of this position is displayed by the plaintiff's argument in *Urofsky v. Gilmore* (2000), a Fourth Circuit case revolving around Virginia's law forbidding state employees from accessing explicitly sexual material on state-owned computers without the permission of a supervisor. The phrase that drives the legal reasoning in the case is "matter of public concern." In a series of decisions the Supreme Court had ruled that if public employees speak out on a matter of public concern, their First Amendment rights come into play and might outweigh the government's interest in efficiency and organizational discipline. (A balancing test is triggered.) If, however, the speech is internal to the operations of the administrative unit, no such protection is available. The *Urofsky* court determined that the ability of employees to access pornography was not a matter of public concern. The plaintiffs, professors in the state university system, then detached themselves from the umbrella category of "public employees" and claimed a special status. They argued that "even if the Act is valid as to the majority of state employees, it violates the . . . academic freedom rights of professors . . . and thus is invalid as to them." In short, we're exceptional.

(4)—*The "Academic freedom as critique" school.* If academics have the special capacity to see through the conventional public wisdom and expose its contradictions, exercising that capacity is, when it comes down to it, the academic's real job; critique—of everything—is the continuing obligation. While the "It's just a job" school and the "For the common good" school insist that the freedom academics enjoy is exercised within the norms of the profession, those who identify academic freedom with critique (because they identify education with critique) object that this view reifies and naturalizes professional norms which are themselves the products of history, and as such are, or should be, challengeable and revisable. One should not rest complacently in the norms and standards pre-supposed by the current academy's practices; one should instead interrogate those norms and make them the objects of critical scrutiny rather than the baseline parameters within which critical scrutiny is performed.

Academic freedom is understood by this school as a protection for dissent and the scope of dissent must extend to the very distinctions and boundaries the academy presently enforces. As Judith Butler (2006a) puts it, "as long as voices of dissent are only admissible if they conform to accepted professional norms, then dissent itself is limited so that it cannot take aim at those norms that are already accepted" (114). One of those norms enforces a separation between academic and political urgencies, but, Butler contends, they are not so easily distinguishable and the boundaries between them blur and change. Fixing boundaries that are permeable, she complains, has the effect of freezing the status quo and of allowing distinctions originally rooted in politics to present themselves as apolitical and natural. The result can be "a form of political liberalism that is coupled with a profoundly conservative intellectual resistance to . . . innovation" (127). From the perspective of critique, established norms are always conservative and suspect and academic freedom exists so that they can be exposed for what they are. Academic freedom, in short, is an engine of social progress and is thought to be the particular property of the left on the reasoning (which I do not affirm but report) that conservative thought is anti-progressive and protective of the status quo. It's only a small step, really no step at all, from academic freedom as critique to the fifth school of thought.

(5)—*The "Academic freedom as revolution" school.* With the emergence of this school the shift from *academic* as a limiting adjective to freedom as an overriding concern is complete and the political agenda implicit in the "For the common good" school and the "Academic freedom as critique" schools is made explicit. If Butler wants us to ask where the norms governing academic practices come from, the members of this school know: they come from the corrupt motives of agents who are embedded in the corrupt institutions that serve and reflect the corrupt values of a corrupt neoliberal society. (Got that?) The view of education that lies behind and informs this most expansive version of academic freedom is articulated by Henry Giroux (2008). The "responsibilities that come along with teaching," he says, include fighting for

> an inclusive and radical democracy by recognizing that education in the broadest sense is not just about understanding, . . . but also about providing the conditions for assuming the responsibilities we have as citizens to expose human misery and to eliminate the conditions that produce it. (128)

In this statement the line between the teacher as a professional and the teacher as a citizen disappears. Education "in the broadest sense" demands positive political action on the part of those engaged in it. Adhering to a narrow view of one's responsibilities in the classroom amounts to a betrayal both of one's political being and one's pedagogical being. Academic freedom, declares Grant Farred (2008–2009), "has to be conceived as a form of political solidarity"; and he doesn't mean solidarity with banks, corporations, pharmaceutical firms, oil companies or, for that matter, universities (355). When university obligations clash with the imperative of doing social justice, social justice always trumps. The standard views of academic freedom, members of this school complain, sequester academics in an intellectual ghetto where, like trained monkeys, they perform obedient and sterile routines. It follows, then, that one can only be true to the academy by breaking free of its constraints.

The poster boy for the "Academic freedom as revolution" school is Denis Rancourt, a physics professor at the University of Ottawa (now removed from his position) who practices what he calls "academic squatting"—turning a course with an advertised subject matter and syllabus into a workshop for revolutionary activity. Rancourt (2007) explains that one cannot adhere to the customary practices of the academy without becoming complicit with the ideology that informs them: "Academic squatting is needed because universities are dictatorships, devoid of real democracy, run by self-appointed executives who serve private capital interests."

So there they are, the five schools of academic freedom, presented somewhat abstractly. A fuller analysis will put flesh on these bones, and as a preview to that analysis, we can consider what the proponents of each school might say about William Robinson, the sociology professor at U.C. Santa Barbara who sent an e-mail to his students comparing Israelis to Nazis and asserting that Martin Luther King would have stood with the Palestinians had he been alive. This time we'll go from left to right, and start with school #5.

(5) — Professors like Giroux and Rancourt would cheer Robinson on. If it is the obligation of academics to oppose tyranny by whatever means are available, and if the means available to teachers include, and are largely limited to, their classrooms, it makes perfect sense to fight the good fight by telling the truth to their students and conscripting them into the army of justice.

(4) — Judith Butler has not, to my knowledge, commented on the Robinson case (she did join over 2,500 scholars in signing a petition supporting him), but she has declared herself on the questions of university divestment from Israeli-affiliated stocks and the boycotting of Israeli universities. She supports both, and in the course of giving her reasons invokes a distinction between "anti-Semitic speech" and "speech which might make a student uncomfortable because it opposes a particular state or set of state policies that he or she may defend" (2003). Butler might well regard Robinson as a teacher who gives his students the gift of such uncomfortable speech and she would certainly resist the drawing of a bright line between political speech and academic speech, on the reasoning that "although extramural expression might not be the same as academic expression, it would seem that they are nevertheless joined as two different ways the public interest is served." And besides, she adds, "it is not possible to distinguish clearly between

expression that is protected as academic freedom and expression that qualifies as extramural expression" (2006a, 124); any such distinction, she more than implies, is likely to mask a politics in the name of pushing politics away.

(3)—Some of those who believe that academic freedom is justified because academics are exceptional beings also believe that academics have the special capacity and responsibility to monitor and correct national opinion. Robinson, they might say, is merely living up to that responsibility when he urges on his students what he takes to be the truth about an important issue. Other proponents of academic exceptionalism, however, are more purist. Their concern is to protect the uniqueness of academic work from the sullying touch of politics and other crassly instrumental forces. They might regard Robinson's e-mail as providing an opportunity for those who are forever poised to invade and colonize the citadel.

(2)—We do not have to guess what the AAUP—the organization that pretty much invented academic freedom in the United States and acts as its watchdog—would say about the Robinson case, because it has said it in a statement cited in the *Santa Barbara Independent* on February 9, 2011: "If an instructor cannot stimulate discussion and encourage critical discussion by drawing analogies or parallels, the vigor and vibrancy of classroom discussion will be stultified." In a separate statement, then AAUP president Cary Nelson (2010) amplified the point: "Historical comparisons are protected by academic freedom, whether or not they were endorsed by a majority of other scholars, even if the analogies are debatable, provocative or reprehensible" (234). I should add that the AAUP was also troubled by the failure of the university to achieve an informal resolution of the Robinson matter, and by alleged procedural irregularities. (This last is no doubt a legitimate concern, given that no university I know of has ever been able to follow its own procedures.)

(1)—And I, as a major stakeholder in the "It's just a job" school? Well I would say that the incident was wrongly characterized by both sides. Those who wanted Robinson disciplined (mostly people from the outside) said that anti-Semitic speech should not be tolerated in the university. Robinson's supporters replied that criticism of Israel was not anti-Semitic and that universities are places where controversies should be aired. But, in my view, the issue is not whether Robinson's e-mail was either anti-Semitic or productive of healthy debate (or both); the issue is whether the e-mail was an academic or a political communication, and that is a question of intention. Was the analogy between Nazis and Israelis offered in the spirit of vigorous discussion or in the spirit of vigorous partisanship? Was it Robinson's intention to initiate an inquiry into the polemical uses of the Nazi-Israeli parallel, just as one might inquire into the polemical history of the cross or the American flag; or was it his intention to affirm the identification and press it on his students?

Fortunately we don't have to speculate about the answer because Robinson (2009) provided it in a speech delivered to the Seventh Annual International Al-Awda Convention in May of 2009. He describes his "growing horror" as the "siege of Gaza" continued for weeks; he resolved, he tells us, to send his students a photo essay that "juxtaposed Nazi atrocities against Jews . . . and Israeli atrocities against Palestinians." He claims that this and other items he sent to the course's e-mail list were to be "material for classroom discussion," but the discussion's direction was dictated in advance by the "commentary" that was written, he boasts, with "passion and conviction," the commentary that begins, "Were Martin Luther King alive on this day." It hardly needs saying that Robinson's passion was not for pedagogy, but for justice. (A passion for justice is of course a good thing; it's just not an academic good thing.) He was moved to send his students these materials not because they provided a perspective on an ongoing conflict—the message was not "here's one way of thinking about what's going on in the Middle East"—but because they represented the truth as he saw it, a truth he wanted his students to take home with them: Palestinians victims, Israelis oppressors.

In his speech, Robinson responds to the charge that his

e-mail was "substantially unrelated" to his course with a statement of incredulity: "How the Israeli invasion of Gaza is unrelated to a course on contemporary global affairs is beyond my comprehension." He has a point, but he misses the more relevant point, as do his detractors. The Israeli occupation of Gaza is without doubt a pertinent and appropriate topic to bring up in the course he was teaching. What was inappropriate was his treating the topic not as a matter of academic study but as the occasion for parading a political judgment that immediately became the course's orthodoxy. That orthodoxy was resisted by two students (out of 80), who filed a complaint with the university. Robinson dismisses them by saying that they "submitted a grievance . . . because they had a different political position than mine." No, they submitted a grievance because they had bought a ticket for a course of academic study and were unhappy to find themselves cast as extras in their teacher's political drama. The difference between a teacher's and his students' political position shouldn't even come into view if the course's materials are being offered as objects of analysis rather than as an invitation to partisan witnessing. (Will you stand with Martin Luther King and me or with the evil Israelis?)

In the debates about academic freedom, one point goes largely uncontroverted. Inquiry the conclusion of which is ordained before it begins is not academic; it is something else, and because it is something else it does not deserve the protection of academic freedom. Professor Robinson's e-mail was something else, not a contribution to scholarly inquiry, but a bypassing of scholarly inquiry in favor of the political agenda to which he was committed. Robinson begins his speech by declaring that "Academic freedom is under attack at the University of California," and throughout he inveighs against a "patent . . . and politicized violation of academic freedom." Politicizing the classroom is what *he* did when he sent the e-mail, and if the offended students politicized in turn, they were shown the way by their professor. If there was an attack on academic freedom at U.C. Santa Barbara, it was his.

William Van Alstyne's comment (2009) on the Robinson case is right on target; when a professor brings material into his class "simply to ventilate some strongly-held view he or she happens to hold, I do not think the event can be glossed as any part of that person's 'academic freedom,' not even a little bit." Larry Alexander (2006) provides a general formulation of the same point when he declares that academic freedom "is a privilege of academics that carries with it a responsibility, namely, to act as academics" (884). If "academics are functioning not as academics, but as political advocates, then they do not merit academic freedom" (884). Exactly!

THE "IT'S JUST A JOB" SCHOOL
Professionalism, Pure and Simple

Underlying each school of academic freedom is an answer to the question, What is education and what is it for? The "It's just a job" school refuses to answer that question in any but professional terms. It is as I said earlier determinedly, some would say perversely, deflationary. That is, it declines to justify education in general or academic freedom more specifically by invoking large abstractions. Instead, the defense of academic freedom flows from a description of the good academics offer—the good of disinterested inquiry—and a determination of exactly what latitude must be allowed professors if they are to be capable of delivering that good. (For whom the good is a good and what the good is good for are questions to be taken up later.)

Academic Freedom and Philosophy
Academic freedom, in this picture, is a subset not of morality or philosophy, but of professionalism, an ideology that emerged in the latter half of the nineteenth century and became regnant in the twentieth. Professionalism is essentially a form of market monopoly. A successful profession is one that has (a) identified, or in some instances created, a need; (b) developed mechanisms for producing the service that meets the need; and (c) persuaded the state, or some ruling elite, to

award it an exclusive franchise for the delivery of the service. You can't simply declare yourself a doctor or lawyer or university professor; those titles are conferred by professional associations that have been recognized by the government as credentialing agencies. The profession controls the flow of licensed practitioners and institutes gate-keeping mechanisms that ensure a scarcity of competence.

The core of the "professionalization project," says Magali Larson (1977), "is the production of professional producers." This project, she adds, "tends to be centered in and allied with the modern university," which "also tends to become the major center for the production of professionally relevant knowledge" (50). Once a profession has been established as the guarantor of relevant knowledge, it will not willingly cede its sphere of control to others. "Only the profession," Eliot Freidson (1970) explains, "has the recognized right to declare . . . 'outside' evaluation illegitimate and intolerable" (71–72), and that is, non-coincidentally, exactly the declaration made by the authors of the 1915 Declaration of Principles of the American Association of University Professors (AAUP): "It is . . . impermissible that the power of determining when departures from the scientific spirit and method have occurred should be vested in bodies not composed of members of the academic profession." Without the liberty to decide what is and is not appropriate within its confines, the profession "cannot rightly render its distinctive and indispensable service to society." Although academic freedom is often celebrated in grand, indeed grandiose, terms, it is at base a guild slogan that speaks to the desire of the academic profession to run its own shop. (The 2012 University of Virginia debacle that saw a president summarily removed by the Board of Visitors and then reinstated in the face of fierce faculty criticism shows that the concerns the 1915 Declaration addresses are still with us.)

I borrow the arguments for this nonphilosophical version of academic freedom from two philosophers, Richard Rorty and Ernest Weinrib. Rorty (1996) asks, "Does Academic Freedom Have Philosophical Presuppositions?" and answers "no." He knows that philosophical pronouncements often accompany invocations of academic freedom, but he regards such formulations as "abbreviations of practices rather than as foundations for practices" (24). That is, it is the history of a practice and not a theory about it that tells us what is central to its performance and what distinguishes a healthy from an unhealthy state of the art. The practice's emergence comes first, after-the-fact theories of it follow.

Those who engage in the practice have internalized its routines, expectations, reward structures, hierarchies, etc. They have not first answered a lot of big questions (What is freedom? What is academic? What is objectivity? What is truth?) and *then* generated a practice:

> To assume that a historian accurately represents the facts as she knows them is to assume that she behaves in the way in which good, honest historians behave; it is not to assume anything about the reality of past events, or the truth-conditions of statements . . . or about any other philosophical topic. (30–31)

A good historian does good history, not good—or necessarily any—theory. If you are doing history and not partisan polemics or hagiography, you want to get the facts right, not because you have some sophisticated account of truth or *any* account of truth, but because that is what historians do. By the same reasoning, if you are doing academic work and not social work or political work, you want to follow the evidence wherever it leads no matter what the unhappy political or social implications, because that's what academics do. And if you want to explain what the content of a practice is, begin not with a theory of it but with a firm grasp of its basic purpose, that is, of the claim it makes to have a place at the table of practices: This is what we do; others do something else.

Ernest Weinrib (1988) calls this perspective on practices "immanent intelligibility," by which he means an understanding of a practice as it is viewed and experienced by insiders who see the field of activity already organized by the purposes that define the enterprise they have joined. His subject is tort law, the law of negligence, and he declares that "Nothing is more senseless than to attempt to understand law from a vantage point entirely extrinsic to it" (952). An extrinsic vantage point would be one from which the features of tort law were explained and evaluated according to the measure of another practice that has its own priorities and values. So you might view tort law from the vantage point of wealth maximization or the spreading out of loss through superfunds and other mechanisms, but that, Weinrib insists, would be to regard tort law as a branch of economics, something it is surely possible to do (an influential school of legal theory is dedicated to doing it), but something that, if done, would distort and underdescribe a practice informed by the goal of redressing wrongs suffered by an individual because of the negligent actions of another.

An account of tort law that did not have that goal at its center would, Weinrib says, leave many of the details of tort law mysterious and its key terms (proximity, causality, due care, etc.) emptied of their operational significance. If the basic features of negligence and redress are not kept steadily in mind, one will slight the constitutive questions of tort law (who suffered what as the result of whose action or failure to act) and another set of questions relevant to another enterprise will take their place. The resulting analysis may call itself tort law—just as professors who do politics or social justice or character improvement still call themselves academics—but it will be so in name only. Moreover it will be difficult to justify the details of the practice, which, in the light of the newly installed "foreign" (Weinrib's word) purpose, will seem superfluous (in a Rube Goldberg way) and hostage to outdated and now extraneous concerns. Justification, if is to be successful, Weinrib (1988) declares, "must be allowed to expand completely into the space it naturally fills" (971). A practice with a justificatory structure that is in good order will be a practice every feature of which can be related immediately and intelligibly to that purpose.

Of course that purpose must be firmly identified and that, according to Weinrib (1988), is the first order of business:

> When we seek the intelligibility of something, we want to know *what* that something is. The search for "whatness" presupposes that something is a *this* and not a *that*, and that it has in other words a determinate content. This content is determinate because it sets the matter apart from other matters and prevents it from falling into the chaos of unintelligible indeterminacy that its identification as a something denies. (958)

So it is important above all to know what you're talking about, to get a fix on its determinate content, and not to confuse the "what" of your enterprise with the "what" of some other or others.

The Rorty-Weinrib description of practices is useful to the "It's just a job" school of academic freedom because it explains why beginning with the distinctive features of the task provides a firm foundation for further reflection and why either elevating the task by attaching it to some exalted moral or political imperative or instrumentalizing it by tying its value to an imported set of justifications (it helps the economy, or improves the quality of national life, or fashions the character of civic-minded citizens) brings confusion rather than clarity to the project of understanding and defending academic freedom. Once the determinate content of the academic task has been circumscribed—in Weinribian terms seen as something, not everything—one can then proceed to specify the degree of freedom necessary to its proper performance. Otherwise the boundaries of freedom will expand with the desires and ambitions of the academic who invokes it.

To be sure, this argument is circular—the stipulation of what is and what is not academic leads to a circumscribed notion of freedom which then can be invoked to exclude certain activities from its umbrella—but the "It's just a job" proponent will claim that the circularity is not vicious but necessary and even virtuous for the reason Weinrib (1988) gives:

Circularity is . . . a strength not a weakness. For if the matter at hand were to be non-circularly explained [and justified] by some point outside it, the matter's intelligibility would hang on something that was not itself intelligible until it was, in turn, integrated into a wider unity. (975)

In short, neither explanation nor justification could be achieved in the face of an infinite regress. Description and justification require circularity if the raison d'être of the enterprise is to be honored. "Criticism on the grounds of circularity implies the superiority of the defective mode of explanation"— the mode that can never come to rest—and "that leaves outside the range of intelligibility the very starting point upon which the whole enterprise depends" (975).

This picture of a practice resting on its own starting point or bottom and resisting incorporation into something higher or more generally compelling has been vigorously challenged both by those who want to march under a more inspiring banner and those who fear that without a grounding in some transcendent truth or universal rationality, academic freedom means little more than the freedom of professors to promote whatever ideas they like, secure in the knowledge that that they need hearken to no tribunal higher than the tribunal of their similarly unconstrained peers. The fear is that if academic work does not rest on a foundation of objectivity, truth, and independent evidence, it is no more than a branch of rhetoric, and the arguments that win the day are simply the arguments urged by the most skillful manipulators of language and symbols. An academic who doesn't believe in truth, objectivity, and a mind-independent reality, it is said, can't possibly be serious. The freedom he claims is the freedom to be frivolous at best and deceptive at worst, and so why should it be granted? The "scholarly ideal," writes philosopher John Searle (1997), "is that of the *disinterested* inquirer engaged in the quest for *objective* knowledge that will have *universal* validity" (209; emphasis in original).

Searle's position is shared by historian Thomas Haskell (1996), who writes explicitly in opposition to Rorty and me. Academic freedom, Haskell declares, is imperiled by "the decay of the epistemological assumptions that originally underwrote the founding of disciplinary communities" (44). Those epistemological assumptions are conveniently listed by Searle (1997): "Reality exists independently of human representations" (201). "Truth is a matter of the accuracy of representation" (203). "A statement is true if and only if the statement corresponds to the facts" (204). "Knowledge is objective" (207). "Intellectual standards are not up for grabs" (207). When Haskell (1996) reports that these assumptions have suffered "decay," he has in mind the assertion by postmodernists, poststructuralists, strong pragmatists, and others that truth, objectivity, and reality are functions of representation rather than checks on it. "Take away the idea of the real," he warns, and "the lesson ceases to be humility and becomes very clearly its opposite"; for if "there is nothing outside language" and "there is nothing real . . . to represent," then one's representations "cannot be inadequate and may as well be asserted with all the force one can muster" (71). The result, he declares, is an academic community in which "nothing at all constrains inquiry, apart from the will of the inquirers," and why, Haskell asks, "should anyone defer to the community's judgment, pay its expenses, or bend over backwards to tolerate its 'findings'" (70)?

Haskell makes two challengeable assumptions. First, he assumes that the use by a practitioner of words like "true," "false," "accurate," "correct," "conclusive," and "wrong" means that he or she is committed not only to those words in their ordinary, task-specific occurrence, but to the "realist" worldview in which they are normatively affirmed; and he also assumes that if the practitioner uses these words but lacks that commitment he or she is at bottom being insincere or cynical So when I say, for example, that I find a reading of *Paradise Lost* to be correct, either I am signing on to the set of interrelated epistemological and ontological propositions Searle lists or I am employing a word ("correct") to which I have no clear title or right.

But such a conclusion puts too much philosophical pressure on a judgment that is internal to a well-developed discipline. When I offer an interpretive judgment, I'm not declaring a position on truth. I'm just pronouncing on a question that has arisen in the course of my engaging in the practice of literary criticism, a practice grounded not in an epistemology to which I must have pledged my allegiance, but in the routines and protocols that are the content of its history, routines and protocols I have internalized in the course of my graduate-school training, my involvement in teaching and research, my participation over the years with other scholars in debates and controversies. It is that *professional*, not philosophical, background that structures my consciousness and my perceptions when I look at the various readings offered of *Paradise Lost* and pronounce one of them "correct," where "correct" means only that given the history of the poem's interpretation and the evidence available to me (evidence being a practice-specific category), I came down here rather than there. Saying "correct" does not oblige me to come up with a full-blown account of exactly what correctness is, or even to have one. Epistemology does not underwrite my judgment; disciplinary competence does; and challenges to my judgment will come not from the epistemological heights, but from the on-the-ground-in-the-trenches perspective of other competent practitioners.

To be sure, in the course of my practicing of literary criticism, abstract, general issues of epistemology will have arisen and I may even have declared a position on them, but when I'm doing literary criticism rather than theorizing about it, my epistemological views are on the shelf, off to one side, beside the point. I take this to be what Searle (1997) means when he says "Realism does not function as a thesis. . . . It is rather the condition of possibility of a certain set of practices" (219). In order to engage in these practices, you have to assume— not declare—the existence of an independent, objective world. Even *assume* is too strong; it suggests a positive act of the mind or will. What I mean by *assume* is closer to "not thinking about" or "taking for granted in an unexamined way." J. Peter Byrne (2004) declares, in the spirit of Haskell, that "academic freedom depends on the assumption that scholars can separate truth from falsehood using disciplinary methods and criteria" (124). That is true only if the notion of an assumption is worn very lightly—as the ticket of entry to an arena, a ticket you can discard when you're done playing that game and have gone on to something else, to another task also undergirded by normative assumptions also unreflectively adhered to.

Haskell's mistake (as I take it to be) is part and parcel of a more general one, the mistake of thinking that whenever you do something you have to have a normative theory of it, even if you are not self-consciously aware of having one. This goes along with the assumption (also a mistake) that we go around the world believing or disbelieving in facts, objectivity, and reality. No, we go around the world encountering facts, experiencing objectivity, and assuming reality. I don't wake up in the morning (and neither do you) and decide "Today I will believe in facts and regard things as real"; instead when I open my eyes (or you, yours) the facts (the window shade, the temperature, my sore back) are just there, and no fancy theory of their instability or perspectival status will dislodge them or make them tremble. And when I go to work and slip into the world of my professional labors, the facts that come along with that world will be perspicuous for me in the same way no matter what I may have concluded at the end of some seminar discussion about the instability of fact.

Haskell's second mistake follows from the first. It is to think that in the absence of a positive commitment to a realist epistemology, the practitioner (of literary criticism or history or legal commentary or anything at all) is without a constraint on his prejudices and desires and there is therefore no bar to his acting as a political rather than a disciplinary agent. (Take away the realist epistemology and it's politics all the way down.) But the constraints Haskell fears losing inhere in the internalized protocols referenced above, the "know-how" that tells a competent member both what she is supposed to do and what she is not supposed to do, not in a way distanced from her consciousness, but in a way that follows from the *content* of her consciousness which is also the content of her perception. As she looks around, the workplace will already be configured by the discipline-relevant dos and don'ts, by the knowledge of what is and is not appropriate behavior in this shop. The work of configuring will not have been done by what David Rabban (1998), a partisan of Haskell's arguments, terms a "developed epistemological position," but by an internalized sense of the practice, a sense that develops in time and is independent of any epistemological position whatsoever (1373). "Metaphysical pictures," as Joseph Raz (2009) points out, do not generate or govern our practices; at best they are "illuminating summaries of central aspects of our practices," and are "accountable to our practices, rather than our practices being accountable to them" (228).

Academic Freedom and Politics

Haskell (1996) acknowledges that I emphasize "the ways in which the community defines the life-world of its members" (74), but he believes that I squander and smother that insight when I argue (as I occasionally do) for the "primacy of the political" (80). But by that I mean only that in every socially organized activity (as teaching and research surely are) the alternative courses of action are always political—in the sense that to take any one of them is to invite an ideologically based disagreement—and that no action one might perform would be entirely independent of controversial substantive propositions.

This, however, is a statement that speaks to the general pervasiveness of the political. What it leaves out are the different forms the political appropriately takes in different arenas of practice. In the world of partisan politics, it is perfectly acceptable, and even regarded as obligatory, to exaggerate, mount ad-hominem attacks, make back-room deals, and generalize wildly from a small statistical sample. But in the academy, to do any of those things is to risk criticism of a kind that calls into question one's status as a legitimate practitioner. There is (famously) something called "academic politics," but it does not include behavior that "real-world" politicians can engage in without danger of being expelled from their club (although it is behavior they criticize each other for; that is part of the conventions).

In short, the unavoidability of the political in a general sense does not authorize the importation into one context of practice a form of politics that is legitimate, and even de rigueur, in some other context of practice. Acting in an academic setting as you would in a partisan-politics setting is a "no-no" because the understanding of what the academic job is, as opposed to the job of getting yourself elected to Congress, includes the understanding that in your efforts to do the job certain kinds of action are not legitimate.

I put it that way because it is important for the "It's just a job" school to be able to justify a firm distinction between academic work and politics (understood as partisan politics) without resorting to metaphysical doctrines of truth, objectivity, etc.; for were the distinction to depend on a moral/philosophical abstraction, that abstraction would be seen as underwriting the academic task which could no longer be described as just a job; it would be an extension of some overarching principle. What the "It's just a job" school says is that the academic work/politics distinction is built into the specification of what the task is; it doesn't have to be added on or sought in philosophy. (To be sure, the academic work/politics distinction is itself a formulation politically inflected; but, according to my argument, it is the "right"—that is, task-appropriate—politics.) If you know (in your disciplinary bones) that what you're supposed to be doing is putting theses, including your own, to the test of rigorous documentation and techniques of falsification, you also and already know that you're not supposed to allow your efforts to be guided or influenced by your partisan ideological desires. Granted, the sequestering of your professional labors from your more general commitments and affiliations can never be total—no matter how hard you try, your personal history will have an effect on the way you conceive of the job—

but that doesn't mean that trying is of no effect. There is all the difference in the world between approaching a class or a research project with the intention of aiding your party and approaching the same class or project with the intention of getting it right, where "getting it right" means coming up with an account or a description or an analysis that does not depend on or derive from any nonacademic allegiances you may happen to have. The results of the two approaches will be different and the difference will be the difference between behaving as an academic and behaving as something else.

The "It's just a job" school regards being on the right side of this difference as an imperative, and it gives that imperative a (clunky) name: academicizing. The imperative of academicizing says that when you bring a topic into a classroom, detach it from its real-world context, where votes are taken or policies urged or rallies organized, and insert it into an academic context where inquiries into its structure, history, significance and value are conducted by means of the traditional methods (textual, archival, statistical, experimental) of humanities, social science, and physical science scholarship. This does not mean that you must stay away from highly charged political topics; only that when you introduce them in the classroom, you ask your students to analyze, describe, and (if appropriate) compare them rather than asking them to take a stand on the issues the topics raise.

The distinction is explained with forceful clarity by Max Weber (1918) in his essay "Science as a Vocation":

> To take a practical political stand is one thing, and to analyze political structures and party positions is another. When speaking in a public meeting about democracy, one does not hide one's personal standpoint. . . . The words one uses in such a meeting are not means of scientific analysis, but means of canvassing votes and winning over others. . . . It would be an outrage, however, to use words in this fashion in a lecture or in the lecture-room. If, for instance, "democracy" is under discussion, one considers

its various forms, analyzes them in the way they function, determines which results for the conditions of life the one form has as compared with the other. . . . But the true teacher will beware of imposing from the platform any political position upon the student, whether it is expressed or suggested. (537)

The "It's just a job "school insists that in the classroom, everything is or should be "under discussion" in the way Weber describes; everything should be academicized. So, to take an example much on everyone's mind these days, it is perfectly okay to discuss the Israeli-Palestinian conflict, its relationship to the Middle East and to World War II, its sources in Zionism and British imperialism and a thousand other things. What is not okay is to lead your students by methods either direct or indirect to come down on one side or the other of the conflict because, as Weber implies, were you to do that, you would no longer be performing as an academic; you would have become a political agent for some cause, as William Robinson was when he sent the Martin Luther King e-mail to his students.

The imperative of academicizing demands the exclusion of no topic from the classroom; anything is potentially a subject matter for academic interrogation. It demands, rather, that whatever topic you have selected for consideration be the object of analysis rather than the vehicle of an agenda. The distinction is not a hard one. Greg Lukanioff (2012) captures it when he says that "teaching a student about the philosophy of Stoicism . . . is not the same as requiring that your students all become classical Stoics" (103). A faculty, explains William W. Van Alstyne (1990), "is employed professionally to test and propose revisions in the prevailing wisdom, not to inculcate the prevailing wisdom in others" (87).

These strictures are often misunderstood as requiring a withdrawal from judgment. But what is required is a withdrawal, or an abstaining from, certain kinds of judgment, not from judgment in general. If you are discussing Francis Fukuyama's *The End of History and the Last Man* and Samuel Huntington's *Clash of Civilizations and the Remaking of World Order* in your class, it is perfectly appropriate and, indeed, obligatory, to assess the strengths and weaknesses of their respective arguments as arguments—Do they cohere? Do they account for the historical evidence? What philosophical traditions do they draw on or continue or challenge or refine?— rather than as policy recommendations students are encouraged to approve or reject.

On the other hand, if you are studying rival accounts of *Paradise Lost* or the English Civil War (where the question might be, is it best explained as a theological, agricultural, economic or military event?), approving one account and rejecting others is well within your pedagogical responsibilities because what you will be approving or rejecting is an analysis and not a call to arms. If, as an instructor, you push the thesis that Satan is the hero of *Paradise Lost,* you're not urging your students to become Satanists; you're urging them to accept the cogency of one interpretation of a literary work rather than another. Of course, even a judgment about who the hero of a literary work is will have behind it (or underneath it) assumptions and presuppositions (about the uses of literature or the nature of heroism) that could be characterized as political in the partisan sense. But those assumptions and presuppositions will not be weighing directly on the academic judgment; they will be deep in the background, and although at a subterranean level they will exert some influence, that influence will be mediated and diffused by the disciplinary protocols that guide and structure the critic's performance.

This is no more than to say that literary studies—like the study of, law, history, philosophy and, yes, politics—is a professional not a moral/political activity. It displays what Andrew Abbott (1988) calls a "formal knowledge system" (53), a system organized by abstractions that correspond to its internal structure, and not to the structure of some socio/economic/political urgency it is obliged to address. The criteria that impel academics, Abbott explains, are "logical consistency and rationality" (as defined by the profession's narrowly conceived field of action), not "efficacy" in the world (53). "Professional knowledge exists, in academia, in a particularly disassembled state that prevents its use" (53). Of course what is disassembled so that it can be the object of academic contemplation can be reassembled by others and put to worldly uses, but, according to the "It's just a job school," that's not the academic's job.

An example. I often say to my classes that given recent court decisions striking down laws against consensual homosexual sex and gay marriage, I can see no legal reason why laws against polygamy shouldn't be struck down too. In saying so, however, I am not speaking out in favor of polygamy or urging the repeal of any laws. I am at most hazarding a prediction of what is likely to follow without indicating approval or disapproval of the outcome I am predicting. Or, to vary the example a bit, let's suppose that polygamy is the subject of a novel, and the interpretive question is whether the novel (and by implication the novelist) is for or against it. As an instructor, I could come down on either side of that question without committing myself to a position on the substantive issue. I would be committing myself to an interpretation of the novel that held polygamy to be either good or bad, not to the proposition that polygamy is either good or bad. On that proposition I would be silent (although if I later became politically involved with the issue, I might appropriate the novel for my polemic).

This, I hasten to add, is not a brief for neutrality. Neutrality is not what the "It's a job" school is about. The trouble with neutrality is that its invocation means that the political perspective that should be absent from the classroom is already present as a measure of judgment and the instructor is just being careful not to tip his or her political hand; if neutrality is being urged as a way of avoiding politics, politics' nose is already under the tent. But if the spirit of academicizing presides over the classroom, the topic under consideration is being interrogated solely within academic categories and one need not call for neutrality because the political (again, in the sense of partisan) implications of the topic have never been allowed to occupy the foreground or even to surface; when things are going properly, there's nothing to be neutral—even-handed—about.

Nor is the question one of balance. Balance is the idea that one can refrain from politicizing the classroom by ensuring that a range of perspectives or approaches is represented. This could mean one of two things, either (1) if you're teaching King Lear or the reform bill of 1832 or evolution, include on your syllabus readings from every position claiming a place in the field; or (2) if you're teaching King Lear or the reform bill of 1832 or evolution, include on your syllabus readings from both conservative and liberal authors.

In either of its forms balance is a bad idea because rather than neutralizing politics, it mandates politics. In version #1 the politics mandated is academic: the instructor is obligated to include every view under the sun even if he considers some of them false or fantastical. But what the instructor should be doing is introducing his students to the views he considers relevant and helpful; the goal, after all, is to get the matter right and, unless the course is a survey of approaches, it's hard to see why requiring balance furthers that goal; the politics of the classroom is or should be meritocratic, not democratic. As Justice David Souter says (in *Regents of the University of Wisconsin System v. Southworth*; 2000), no one claims "that that the University is somehow required to offer a spectrum of courses to satisfy a viewpoint neutrality requirement."

In version #2, the politics mandated is, well, politics. It says that if you have a text by Marx or Keynes on your reading list you must balance it with a text by von Hayek or Milton Friedman. The reasoning is that the classroom is a space where the forces of the left and right contend for mastery and the instructor should be a referee or honest broker. This is the confusion—between a "public meeting" and academic inquiry—Weber warns against, a confusion the proponents of balance eagerly embrace. A text should be introduced into the classroom because the teacher believes it illuminates the material, not because of the perceived political affiliation of the author. The bringing in of opposing political views rather than balancing—and supposedly sanitizing—politics elevates politics to the classroom's first concern. If Professor Robinson had, in the name of balance, included in his e-mail materials depicting the Palestinians as rabid jihadists, and then asked his students to choose between these two political caricatures (as opposed to studying them as caricatures), he would not have cured the disease but fed it.

Some teachers think they can have their politics and eat it too by flagging their views up front. They say, I let my students know where I stand on the political issues of the day so that they can discount my biases. The "It's just a job" school regards this strategy as particularly dishonest. It's like an advance get-out-of-jail-free card, a claimed immunization from a virus it in fact introduces, or like a parent saying to a child, "Now don't be influenced by my opinion just because I'm your mother." Every child and student knows what he or she is supposed to do next: come to the preapproved conclusions while pretending that they have been arrived at independently. Announcing your political preferences as a supposedly prophylactic gesture is a sure way to surrender the classroom to politics.

The points I have made in the previous paragraphs follow from the core tenets of the "It's just a job" school. If the instructor's task is limited to introducing students to traditions of inquiry and equipping them with the skills necessary to move around in those traditions—no more, no less—it follows that introducing political issues in the classroom as issues to be voted on rather than as objects of study is not part of the task. As Erica Goldberg and Kelly Sarabyn (2011) explain, "there is little justification for affording *academic* protection to decisions that are not academic in nature, but rather ideological," that is, "motivated by the goal of altering students'... values ... as a way of effecting political or social change" (240). Debating political issues with a view to deciding them and then taking the actions your decision dictates is a valuable and necessary activity in a democracy, but it is not an academic activity and therefore it does not deserve protection under the doctrine of academic freedom.

THE "FOR THE COMMON GOOD" SCHOOL
Academic Freedom,
Shared Governance,
and Democracy

I have several times hinted, as I did at the end of the previous chapter, that academic concerns and the concerns of democracy may come apart, and I wish now directly to consider the extent to which "academic" and "democratic" are overlapping and/or distinct categories. In raising this question, I shall be preparing the way for a discussion of the "It's for the common good" school of academic freedom.

Academic Freedom and Shared Governance
The tension between democratic and academic values is illustrated by the debate over whether academic freedom requires shared governance, a form of institutional organization that is democratic in spirit insofar as its goal is to spread the franchise and the responsibility for decision making as widely as possible. Can academic freedom flourish only in settings where the faculty is a full or nearly full partner in the making of decisions, not just decisions about personnel and curricular matters but decisions about anything arguably related to instruction and research? To this question Larry Gerber (2001) responds with a firm "yes" in the title of a widely read essay: "'Inextricably Linked': Shared Governance and Academic Freedom." It should be said that Gerber resists any facile linking of shared gover-

nance to democracy; he points out, as others do, that although democracy is egalitarian and values all voices equally, academic practices demand judgment and the ranking of voices according to the contribution each makes, or fails to make, to the enterprise. Therefore "it is misleading to base the faculty claim to a primary role in academic governance on strictly democratic principles" (Gerber 2010, 22).

Instead, Gerber contends, we should base the justification for shared governance as an essential element of academic freedom on the notion of "expertise," and he finds support for this position in statements made by the fledgling AAUP in the early decades of the last century. Its 1915 Declaration of Principles declares that it would be "unsuitable to the dignity of a great profession that the initial responsibility for the maintenance of professional standards should not be in the hands of its own members." In a 1920 report on the role of faculty in governance, the same organization insists "that in the matter of the determination and carrying out of educational policies, the members of the faculty are the experts, and should usually have the principal voice in the decision." Citing these and similar declarations, Gerber (2010) concludes that "Academic freedom . . . requires a government system in which faculty expertise . . . is the determining factor in institutional decisions affecting academic matters" (13).

The "It's just a job" school will be sympathetic to this line of reasoning when it is modestly asserted, for that school conceives of the academy as a guild rather than a holy calling, and recognizes as natural the desire of guild members to regulate their own affairs. The difficulty enters with the question of what, exactly, is the scope of a faculty's "own affairs"? What, in Gerber's terms, is an institutional decision "affecting academic matters"? An expansive view of the matter would answer "every decision" and one can imagine how that claim to shared governance at every level of the operation might be justified. After all, the location of a computing center far from her office might be experienced by a professor as an impediment to her research. "Why didn't they consult me?," she might ask, as might another professor who has determined that placing parking lots on the perimeter of the campus costs him a good 10 hours a week in research time. Examples could easily be multiplied, and they would all point in the same direction: because anything done on a campus ultimately affects academic matters, everything done on a campus should be done only after the faculty has been consulted, and not just in a pro forma way.

But this argument (which I am not attributing it to Gerber) goes beyond the faculty-expertise justification of shared governance—we are scholars and so scholarly judgment belongs to us—and substitutes for it an assertion of faculty supremacy—we are the heart of the university and so when others in the university think to do something, they must check with us first. A budget officer or a maintenance supervisor or an athletic director or even a president may be under the misapprehension that she has a sphere of authority and along with it responsibilities the discharge of which will be monitored by her superiors in the organization; but in fact, the shared-governance apostles will say, she works for the faculty and is answerable to faculty judgments. This is what Professor Isidor Rabi famously told Dwight Eisenhower when, as president of Columbia University, Eisenhower referred to professors as employees. "Excuse me, sir," said Rabi, "the faculty are not employees of the university. The faculty are the university."

In the same spirit, faculty members at Idaho State University protested when, as a response to severe budget cuts, the president unveiled a plan in 2009 to reorganize the university by reducing the number of colleges from seven to five with a view, it was claimed, to trimming administrative costs. A majority of the faculty opposed the changes, but in the end the president implemented them and received the approval of the Idaho State Board of Education. Protests continued and in May 2011 the AAUP issued a report siding with the faculty:

> Rather than allow the senate, other duly constituted
> faculty bodies, or faculty selected representatives to
> participate appropriately in important decision-making

processes concerning the organization of the university and the shape of faculty governance, the administration repeatedly, and over the objections of the faculty's representatives, chose to make these major decisions based on the recommendations of task forces selected by the administration and dominated by administrators. (Schmidt 2011)

The accusation, in short, is that administrative decisions were being made by administrators. What will they think of next? To be sure, it is entirely possible that the president's reorganization was ill-advised for all the reasons given by the faculty, but it is his, not the faculty's, job to set grand plans in motion and then to be judged by the result. (This same conflict between administrative initiatives and faculty insistence on fully shared governance is being played out as I write at New York University, where resistance to expansion both in Greenwich Village and abroad has led some units to produce a vote of no-confidence in the university president.)

One can understand why faculty members would wish to have a strong voice in every decision a university administration makes. But what is the content of that wish? Is it merely a desire for power or is it undergirded by the conviction that strong faculty governance is a necessary ingredient in the production of good teaching and good scholarship? Gerber (2001) would answer the latter, for he believes that faculty "need affirmative authority to shape the environment in which they carry out their responsibilities" (23). The "It's a job" school will reply "no" and insist that the form of management prevailing in a university is logically independent of the quality of the work produced in its classrooms and laboratories. Graeme Moodie (1996) makes the point concisely. "Logically speaking, scholarly freedom neither depends upon nor necessarily requires academic freedom in the sense of self-government or rule by academics" (143). "One can imagine," Moodie adds, "some scope for independent scholarly work . . . even in highly autocratic institutions" (143). You can have a top-down corporate style of management or a bottom-up fully consultative form of management and teaching and scholarship could flourish or fail to flourish in either. What is crucial is not the chain of command or who gets to vote on what, but whether the classroom, the research laboratory, personnel decisions, and curricular decisions are insulated from the illegitimate pressures brought to bear by donors, grantors, and political operatives. The environment (to use Gerber's word) that counts is the close-up environment, the one intimately tied to the performance of academic work. The larger environment, including everything from the location of food courts to the number of associate vice provosts (a position I once occupied) may have some impact on academic work, but it will not be decisive, and the impact it might have does not justify handing over big chunks of governance to the faculty.

In making this argument, the "It's just a job" school takes a cue from Immanuel Kant's brief 1784 tract "What Is Enlightenment?" In it, Kant distinguishes between the public use of reason—"the use that anyone as a scholar makes of reason before his peers in the literate world"—and the private use of reason—the reason a person exercises "in a civic post or office that has been entrusted to him." The former, Kant declares, must always be free, but the latter can legitimately be constrained by the requirements of the post or office. Neither use of reason necessarily clashes with the other; they can be performed in the same political space. Indeed, a man can be employing one kind of reason in the morning and engaging in the other in the afternoon:

> A pastor is bound to instruct his . . . congregation in accordance with the symbol of the church he serves . . . but as a scholar he has complete freedom, indeed even the calling, to impart to the public all of his carefully considered and well-intentioned thoughts concerning mistaken aspects of that same symbol.

The freedom one enjoys as a scholar is not compromised by the restrictions placed on one's behavior as a functionary in a bureaucracy. Kant (1798) contends that when a man man is speaking as a scholar to other scholars, he "must be conceived as free and subject only to the laws given by reason" (43), but when the government asks that he obey generally applicable laws pertaining to "public peace," the same man is obliged to assent. (This distinction will be pertinent when we turn in a later chapter to the topic of academic freedom and public employee law.)

The correspondence between Kant's situation (he writes in a state ruled by an absolute monarch) and the situation of a faculty member who labors in a university where the marching orders come from the top is not perfect, but the general point holds: the production of good scholarship does not depend on the political organization of the university within which scholarly inquiry is conducted; no matter what the lines and direction of authority might be, scholarly work can flourish "as long as the government does not see fit to intervene in scholarly discussions" (Kant 1798, 57).

Shared governance, then, is not necessary to the flourishing of academic work. But the question can be turned around: Will academic work flourish under a regime of shared governance? Not really, says James Duderstadt (2004), former president of the University of Michigan. He explains that at a time of "profound changes" in higher education, "the academic tradition of extensive consultation, debate and consensus building before any substantive decision is made or action taken poses a particular challenge" to the goal of getting something done (143). The challenge is intensified, Duderstadt asserts, by the profile of those who call most loudly for shared governance. "It is rare," he says, "that a distinguished faculty member will spare the time from productive scholarship" to serve on an endless round of committees. Instead, "faculty members with an axe to grind are [the ones] drawn to academic politics, frequently distracting faculty governance from substantive issues to focus instead on their pet agendas" (149). Although Duderstadt agrees with those who say "that faculty should have . . . a sustained voice in matters pertaining to knowledge production," he finds that it is "difficult to get faculty . . . to focus on those areas clearly within their unique competence," and he concludes that the "tradition of shared governance in which power is shared more or less equally among all potential decision makers, is cumbersome and awkward at best" (145). "Not everything," he remarks drily, "is improved by making it more democratic" (149).

George Keller (2004) presents an even harsher view. He observes that a "majority of professors cling to medieval privileges while demanding modern trade union benefits." That is, although faculty members "have the rights of employees of a purposive corporation," they resist "the obligation to give up control over their time for use toward a corporate goal." They accept the benefits of the purposive corporation, but insist that the only purposes they will be responsive to are their own. The effect, Keller observes, is to "create a status with special privileges, a status with the autonomy of a community member, the security of a corporate employee, and the obligations of neither" (169). Two questions immediately suggest themselves: Who wouldn't wish such a status? And why should any institution grant it? (The desire to be on both sides of the table by claiming management rights and employee benefits at the same time was denied by the Supreme Court in *N.L.R.B v. Yeshiva University*, 1980.)

A member of the "It's just a job" school will tend to agree with Duderstadt's and Keller's strictures, but there will be a caveat: much depends on the nature and size of the institution. If the goal is to establish conditions that facilitate the work of teaching and scholarship, the question of governance will be an instrumental one, not a moral or philosophical one. (Once again the perspective of the "It's just job" school will be deflationary.) What helps get the job done? "Shared governance" seems not to be the answer in a large school like the University of Michigan, but it could well be the answer in a small college with a faculty focused on teaching and a tradition of close relationships between teachers and students, in and out of class. At the university level, Keller (2004) declares, "shared governance increasingly is a failure," but, he acknowledges, "it can work quite effectively at smaller institutions if there is mutual understanding, mutual respect, and generosity of spirit" (172). Given the variables Keller lists—"whether a school is small or huge, religiously sponsored or secular, rich or struggling, liberal arts or research-oriented, two-year or four-year, public or private"—his conclusion seems exactly right (171). No one size fits all; "pluralism rather than standardization should become the norm in academic governance" (171).

Academic Freedom and Democracy

This seems to be just common sense, but it will not be heeded if issues of governance are moralized, if the question of who gets to vote on what is asked not in the spirit of ensuring that the enterprise can keep moving forward—classes taught, curricula kept up to date, research projects completed—but in the spirit of affirming and claiming constitutional, even divine, rights. Governance is a means, not an end, and the moment it becomes an end, the moment you are more concerned with being political master than with getting the job done, the point of the job—to seek truth in the company of inquiring students—will have been displaced by a political concern.

This is a particular danger when the political concern is an attractive one, which is of course the case with democracy. Tying academic freedom to the flourishing of democracy may seem a way of supporting its claims—see, academic freedom is good for democracy; how can anyone be against it?—but the "It's just a job" school will argue the opposite: once academic freedom is justified because of its supposed contribution to democracy, the question put to it changes, no longer how will this or that version of academic freedom advance the doing of academic work, but how will this or that version of academic freedom advance the project of democracy?

That is the question Robert Post (2012), a leading spokesperson of the "For the common good" school, asks in a recent book, *Democracy, Expertise, and Academic Freedom: A First Amendment Jurisprudence for the Modern State.* The argument of Post's book develops from an implicit tension between the first two words in its title, *democracy* and *expertise*. The relationship between democracy and the First Amendment is often represented by the metaphor of the marketplace of ideas. In a democracy government does not have a proprietary purchase on truth and can neither monopolize the conversation nor dictate its course. The state is only one voice among many and it must allow all voices into the marketplace where, in the fullness of time, the truth will emerge. As Post observes, at the heart of the First Amendment is "an egalitarian commitment" (10) to the equality of speakers and their ideas.

Equality, however, is a concept foreign to the disciplines whose job it is to produce expertise. If what you are after is knowledge that is reliable and authoritative, those in the business of fashioning it must be credentialed and held to professional standards. Exclusion of voices is necessary. On its face, then, the knowledge industry—the academy—cannot be understood as a subset of democracy and the First Amendment, for, as Post (2012) observes, "the production of expert knowledge . . . depends on the continuous exercise of peer judgment to distinguish meritorious from specious opinions" and therefore "expert knowledge requires exactly what normal First Amendment doctrine prohibits" (9). J. Peter Byrne (1989) makes the same point: "Democratic values exist in tension with academic freedom because they insist that the university . . . be measured by standards other than academic competence" (282).

But Post mounts an argument that binds the two together. Taking his cue (as almost everyone does) from the AAUP's 1915 Declaration, he observes that democracy can flourish only if the citizens in a democratic society are in possession of the expertise that will enable them to make wise decisions. They must acquire what Post (2012) calls "democratic competence." "Democratic competence refers to the cognitive empowerment of persons within public discourse, which in part depends on their access to disciplinary knowledge" (34). Post notes that in the area of commercial advertising, the courts have already extended First Amendment protection to "the flow of information so as to enhance the quality of public decision-making" (42). It makes perfect sense, he argues, to extend the same protection "to the disciplinary practices by which expert knowledge"—[as opposed to mere commercial knowledge] "is created" (55).

The courts have not yet done this, but the path, Post (2012) believes, is open. If democratic competence is accepted as a First Amendment value (because the responsible exercise of First Amendment rights requires it), and if democratic competence is fashioned in large part by academic institutions, then academic freedom—the freedom to engage in that fashioning without political interference—is more than the slogan of a guild that wishes to be left to its own devices. Here is the sequence of reasoning: Because "academic freedom safeguards the creation of disciplinary knowledge within universities" (61), and because disciplinary knowledge is a chief ingredient of democratic competence, and because without democratic competence democratic decision making rests on the shifting sands of public opinion, academic freedom merits the status of a constitutional value and a value to which academics have a constitutional right. The conclusion may seem startling but Post finds it implicit in the words of Justice Felix Frankfurter in *Wieman v. Updegraff* (1952):

> To regard teachers . . . as the priests of our democracy is . . . not to engage in hyperbole. It is the special task of teachers to foster those habits of open-mindedness and critical inquiry which alone make for responsible citizens, who in turn make possible an enlightened and effective public opinion.

As a public relations argument for academic freedom, this has a lot going for it. You will remember that we began in chapter 1 by asking why academics should be granted exemptions and privileges not enjoyed by workers in other fields. Post has an answer. Academics should be free from monitoring and interference because democracy can function properly only if the knowledge they produce is available to citizens. What professors want and what democracy needs come together quite neatly. Paul Horwitz (2007) makes a similar argument under the rubric of "universities as First Amendment institutions."

Nevertheless members of the "It's just a job" school will demur, in part for the same reason that leads them to reject the argument that academic freedom and academic work require shared governance: a variable feature has been misidentified as the essential thing. Shared governance, as I have said, is a possible principle of organization in the university; but the central task of the university—the advancement of knowledge—can proceed no matter what form the bureaucracy takes, as long as the independence of academic judgment is protected. In short, shared governance is not a necessary condition for the realization of the academic project.

Nor is the realization of the academic project a necessary condition for the flourishing of democracy. Although the knowledge produced by academic expertise may be helpful to the democratic project, the democratic project can get along without it. There are other resources that will contribute to the formation of informed citizens—parents, churches, free libraries, political discussion groups, newspapers, high-level journals, the internet, public television, National Public Radio, documentaries, popular culture, folk wisdom, common sense.

Elitism is the word that comes to mind here, and it is a concept unabashedly embraced in the AAUP's 1915 Declaration, where, you will recall, academic institutions are said to serve as a necessary "check" on "the unconsidered impulses of popular feeling." No academics, no wisdom is the message, and that message, presented subliminally by Post (2012), leads in the end to the assertion of academic exceptionalism, the idea that not only are academics better credentialed than other people, they are better. It is one thing to say that academic work should not be hostage to popular opinion. It is quite another to say that popular opinion is unredeemable unless academics correct and refine it. The first statement affirms the necessary independence of academic work from external controls.

The second raises academics to the status of cultural saviors, as Byrne (2004) seems to do when he defends giving "greater free speech rights to professors than to other citizens" because they provide "knowledgeable and complex assertions about the world and persons in ways not possible on street corners or on television." Indeed, Byrne adds, "we lack enough cultural institutions outside of colleges and universities to make most speech fruitful" (139). Either give academics special speech privileges, the argument goes, or the entire democratic project goes downhill. That is quite a claim and, in my view, one that cannot be cashed in.

But the main objection to the "academic freedom is necessary for democracy" thesis is not that it is hubristically elitist (although it surely is), but that it is one more way of locating the value of academic work in the service it performs for another enterprise. "It's good for democracy" is just another, albeit more appealing, version of "it's good for the state's bottom line" or "it's good for the fashioning of character." The implication is that if academic work and the freedom to do it properly are to be justified, the measure of justification will come from elsewhere. Now it may be true that academic work makes a contribution to these other enterprises (although each of them will survive without it), but that is not the reason academics engage in it. That is, academics do not set out to aid democracy or help build the economy or produce good citizens; these things may contingently happen, but achieving them is not the point. The point is to go down intellectual paths wherever they lead, to challenge received wisdom, to confer analytical skills, to build systems of analysis, to formulate and test hypotheses. In the course of doing all these things, desirable unintended consequences may ensue, but they cannot be cited as the justification of an activity that did not have them in contemplation.

With apologies to Keats, justification, justification, the very word "is like a bell / to toll me back" ("Ode to a Nightingale"). Justification is where most discussions of academic freedom begin and end, and for an obvious reason: the claim of academic freedom is so extraordinary that a case must be made for it, and making the case always involves going outside the precincts of academic activity in an effort to persuade nonacademics that academic privileges make sense. An argument like Post's or Byrne's succeeds in doing that but ends up abandoning an internal justification of academic freedom, a justification that flows from the nature of the task rather than from the contribution the task makes to other tasks. An internal justification of academic freedom is all the "It's just a job" school can offer—this is the job and these are the conditions we require to do it properly. But the minimalism of that justification (not really a justification at all) is purchased at the price of not having anything to say when a legislator or a businessman or a taxpayer asks "Yes, I see why that's good for you, but why is it good for *me*?" The "It's just a job" school's inability—indeed unwillingness–to answer that question is at once its greatest weakness and its greatest strength. It is its greatest weakness because it gives up on the public relations task before it is even begun; it is its greatest strength because, in refusing the challenge of public/political justification, it reaffirms the independent value of what academics do, and provides a secure, because wholly internal, justification of allowing them to do it freely.

PROFESSIONALISM VS. CRITIQUE
The Post-Butler Debates

Justification can take the form either of pointing to a good result of the practice being justified or of pointing to the special virtue of those who perform it. The latter strategy is adopted by those who, in the spirit of the American Association of University Professors (AAUP) 1915 Declaration of Principles, stress not only the intellectual capabilities, but the moral and even spiritual superiority of academics, and argue that, because of that superiority, academics should be free from the restrictions imposed on others.

The argument depends on an equivocation between the concepts of "different" and "special." Burton R. Clark (1971) says of "academic man" that he "is a special kind of professional, a type characterized by a particularly high need for autonomy" (241). In this statement *special* seems to refer to the kind of work being done rather than to the character of the person doing it. The reasoning, which we have met before, is that because the academic task is to discover truths rather than adhere to truths already established, those assigned that task must be free to go in whatever direction their research suggests. In his next sentence, however, Clark veers in the direction of attributing the special nature of the situation to the special quality of the researcher: "To be innovative, to be critical of established ways, these are the commitments of the academy and the impulses of scientific and scholarly roles that press for unusual autonomy" (241).

In a single sentence, Joan Scott (1996) joins Clark in splitting the difference between the institution and the practitioner as the deserving recipient of special consideration: "Academic freedom protects those whose thinking challenges orthodoxy; at the same time the legitimacy of the challenge—the proof that the critic is not a madman or a crank—is secured by membership in a disciplinary community" (163). The part of the sentence before the semicolon confers a protected status on those who are inclined to challenge orthodoxy; the freedom is properly theirs because of the kind of persons they are. In the part of the sentence after the semicolon, the freedom belongs only to those who are embedded in the discipline and responsive to its norms; the lone heroic figure speaking truth to power (a favored image of those who argue for an expansive understanding of academic freedom) is replaced by the professional who speaks the kind of truth the institution defines and fosters.

The tension between regarding the institution as special and regarding the individual teacher/researcher as special is a permanent feature of debates about academic freedom. Much hangs on it. If the institution's norms establish the scope of academic freedom, the individual teacher/researcher is constrained in what he or she can properly say or do. If the individual teacher/researcher is constrained only by his or her sense of which orthodoxies pose a threat to genuine freedom, the institution's norms lose their normative status, become the object of critique, and flouting them can be declared a moral obligation. At that moment, all the disciplinary brakes are off and we are headed in the direction of "academic freedom as revolution" territory.

The stakes in this debate are brilliantly on display in point-counterpoint essays written by Robert Post and Judith Butler. Post (2006) explains why it is a mistake to regard academic freedom as a subset of First Amendment rights. Every citizen, he reminds us "holds First Amendment rights," but "only faculty . . . possess academic freedom." It follows, he continues, that this particular freedom "must derive from values that attach to the distinct professional role of the scholar" (63). It cannot, therefore, be attached to the scholar as an individual; it is a "corporate" freedom which does not liberate the faculty member, but constrains him: "The function of academic freedom is not to liberate individual professors from all forms of university regulation, but to ensure that faculty within the university are free to engage in the professionally competent forms of inquiry and teaching" (64). (This is a version of Graeme Moodie's "activity freedom"; Moodie 1996). Academic freedom, Post declares, has never protected "the autonomy of professors to pursue their own individual work, free from university restraints."

In Post's view—a view I share—academic freedom is best understood "as the unimpeded application of professional norms of inquiry" (2006, 70). Were we to "conceptualize academic freedom on the model of individual First Amendment rights possessed by "all 'citizens in a free society,'" we could "neither explain the basic structure of faculty obligations"—the particular things faculty members are responsible for doing— "nor provide a trenchant defense" of academic freedom (62). For a defense to be persuasive, the freedom academics claim to enjoy must be seen to follow from the nature of the task academics pledge themselves to perform. They are free (within limits) to do that, not free to do anything that comes into their heads. Were universities unable to hold faculty members to professional standards, they "could not function" (70); for absent such standards, there would be no bounds to the freedom of faculty members and the university as a coherent and cohesive unit would fly apart.

Moreover, given that professional standards are fully known only to those who have internalized them—to insiders—outsiders cannot be trusted to pass judgment on academic performance; for, as Post argues, not "having been socialized into the knowledge and practice of professional norms," outsiders "will tend to enforce standards that are extrinsic to the profession," standards derived not from the university's mission, but from "popular political beliefs" (71). It is not just that popular political beliefs should not be allowed to distort academic work; they should not be taken note of at all (except as objects of analysis). Their absence, both as an influence from the outside and as a perspective entertained on the inside, is constitutive of academic work. External economic/political interests are not only dangers to the self-determination of a profession vulnerable to outside takeovers; they mark the boundaries in relation to which the profession understands itself to be what it is and not something else. Teaching styles, Post observes, vary, but the "essential point is that a professor's pedagogical approach must educate, rather than indoctrinate, students" (81). The point is essential not as a constraint on the academy (that would be a weak understanding), but as a definition of the academy. Were a "professor's pedagogical approach" to indoctrinate, it wouldn't be a professor's *pedagogical* approach. The academy is a place where political norms—perfectly respectable and necessary in their place—don't belong because professional norms fill the landscape.

In her reply to Post, Butler (2006a) inquires into the status of those norms. She begins by observing that they didn't drop from the sky. What Post in her view regards as a set of fixed and stable professional constraints, she sees "as historical conventions . . . that emerge, transform, and sometimes disappear, become the sites for consequential epistemological debate, and are subjected to repeated scrutiny as academic fields seek to renew themselves in light of new demands on knowledge" (107). We have a choice, Butler says, between two views of academic norms and two views of academic freedom; *"if we are to preserve academic freedom, either professional norms are necessary restraints that we ought not to question or professional norms have to bear internal scrutiny"* (112; emphasis in original). She declares for the second of these alternatives, and argues that if "voices of dissent are only admissible if they conform to accepted professional norms, . . . new fields or disciplinary paradigms" will fail to emerge. Therefore, she concludes, "To question existing professional norms . . . must be part of any bona fide academic inquiry" (115).

When Butler calls professional norms "historical conventions," we should hear a silent "mere" before the phrase. A convention is by definition an artificial construct; a conventional norm is one that emerged in history against a background of material/political/cultural conditions; when those conditions change, it is possible (and perhaps likely) that the norms will change too. Butler observes that Post's account of professional norms follows from the AAUP's 1915 Declaration. Against that background, she says, Post's "argument is persuasive." But 1915 was a long time ago. "Are there," she asks, "no new circumstances that call for a revision of the theory?" She observes that the traditional model of academic freedom (which Post elaborates and defends) assumes a science-based "quantitative augmentation of knowledge" that is presently not accepted by the "prevailing paradigms" in the humanities or social sciences (110–11). Academic freedom, she continues, has to be understood in relation to the "kinds of activities that a faculty member is free to perform," and those activities will reflect the models of knowledge production presently presupposed in the academy. It follows, then, that an account of academic freedom and its norms should "agree with the way knowledge is pursued now" (111). The norms Post invokes are out of date; they are unresponsive to the new epistemologies that have emerged since their formulation almost a hundred years ago.

Now this is a powerful point, but it finally cuts differently than Butler thinks it does. First of all, it is a point Post (2006) himself makes when he says that "the distinction between education and indoctrination is largely internal to academic standards" (81). That is, the distinction is not found in some independent, abstract calculus and then applied to the academy; rather, the academy's practices declare it; if you want to know the source of the distinction, you look to the practices and not to anything more foundationally legitimating. (This, you will recall, is Rorty's argument.)

That, however, is precisely Butler's complaint. In the second of her debates with Post, she asks "What, if anything, legitimates" academic norms like the distinction between education and indoctrination (Butler 2009, 774)? The answer, which is implied in her question, is "nothing" and it is Post's answer too. Academic practices and the norms that configure them rest on themselves (again Butler's complaint), and because they do they must not be relaxed; for if they were—if they were abandoned or expanded as Butler wants them to be—they would no longer be what they are. And by the same reasoning, were we to derive our understanding of academic freedom from the now "prevailing paradigms of knowledge" (Butler 2006a, 111), paradigms that tend to soften and blur any distinction between education and politics, the derivation would be impossible because in those paradigms (deconstruction, postmodernism, antifoundationalism), there is no room for a sealed-off academic space within whose confines one might claim to be free. If the contingent (and revisable) nature of line-drawing is not only a principle one affirms in theory, but a reason actively to distrust and disregard any and all lines that have been drawn, no institution can retain its shape long enough to be capable of doing any work; it will always be in the process of being dissolved by critique; the ground beneath your feet will continually be shifting. The epistemology underlying the traditional account of academic freedom, the epistemology that "assumes a quantitative augmentation of knowledge" (110), may no longer be good currency in some philosophy departments, but if you want there to be an academy that has its own shape and is its own place, it is the epistemology you must presuppose. It may seem paradoxical or even quixotic, but the maintenance of the categories of the academic and of academic freedom requires the assumption of an account of knowledge that some academic disciplines have declared out of date.

This is not to say that you must positively affirm an epistemology that you in (theoretical) fact reject. Hypocrisy is not what is being counseled. Affirming or rejecting epistemologies is what you do in philosophy seminars; when you're engaged in a practice, you fall in with—as opposed to actively espousing—the epistemology its methods and protocols declare. To return to Rorty's point about the discipline of history, you can be a hard-core denier of the independence of fact in the morning, and be a serious inquirer after historical fact in the afternoon. You can believe, as a theorist, that, as David Rabban (1998) puts it (he rehearses a thesis he rejects), "it is impossible to make meaningful statements about an external world," but then, as a practitioner, set about making, and standing by, a whole host of statements you unproblematically warrant as meaningful.

Once, when I presented these arguments to an academic audience, a distinguished member of the host faculty came up to me afterward and delivered a one-word judgment: "Quaint." By "quaint" I took her to mean dated, old-fashioned, nostalgic, and retrograde. She was right, but lots of the conventions of thought we hold onto are like that; they emerged in time and brought with them forms of activity that would disappear if they were discarded. Sometimes we decide to keep them in place even though we know that they could not be justified by the new arguments we have learned to make because we don't want to lose those forms. For example, it is now recognized in advanced academic quarters that the distinction between speech and action on which the First Amendment depends ("sticks and stones may break my bones, but names will never hurt me") does not stand up under examination. But even those of us who question the distinction as a matter of theory do not urge its abandonment in practice because we do not want the policies it renders intelligible—the policy, for example, of not punishing words that wound unless they are libelous, treasonous, or intentional incitements to violence—to disappear. Against our nuanced philosophical knowledge, we stick with formulations that we recognize as quaint. And, in the same way, if we want to continue to enjoy the pleasures of academic work, we must quaintly attribute to that kind of work an independence and autonomy that is disallowed by our current theories.

Butler (2006a) talks as if she were willing to forgo those pleasures for the greater pleasures of political engagement, and thus to forgo the distinctiveness that separates the academy from the larger world. But I'm not so sure. Here is a sentence in which she makes her usual point about the historicity of norms: "Post's view," she says, "fails to acknowledge that norms are themselves in vital and constant tension with one another, that existing conflicts among norms are very often the theme and subject of academic work, and that innovation in academic life depends in part on invoking and elaborating new norms over and against established fields of knowledge" (115). Right in the middle of this sentence are the noun-phrases "academic work" and "academic life," casually uttered as if they named entities the features of which are generally known. That of course is right. We do know what we mean when we say "academic work" and "academic life." But by her own arguments Butler is not allowed to know that, and she is certainly not allowed to trade on that knowledge when writing sentences like this one. Remember, her argument is that because Post's professional norms are always being contested and questioned, they cannot be invoked in an effort to specify what does and does not belong in the academy; their history, she says repeatedly, "is not over." It would follow then that she shouldn't be able to refer to academic work and academic life without putting the phrases in quotes—without, that is, indicating that the phrases stand for something provisional and on the wing (as Jacques Derrida does when he performs "writing under erasure"). But she does refer to them unproblematically throughout the essay because she knows—although it is not a knowledge she can admit to having—that amidst the ongoing contestation of norms, something abides, and that something is the general project of engaging in a kind of work that is distinctive, even though the precise nature of its distinctiveness is often a matter of debate.

When Butler reports (correctly) that members of an academic department will sometimes disagree "on the very method and norm by which . . . work ought to be evaluated"

(119), we have to ask what kind of disagreement is then occurring? The answer is an *academic* disagreement, the kind of disagreement appropriate to the academy, and not, for example, a disagreement between those who think that work in the academy should reflect Republican Party values and those who think that work in the academy should reflect Democratic Party values. No department meeting will ever be the location of that disagreement, again something Butler knows and acknowledges (albeit implicitly) when she confidently references academic work and academic life. Even when norms are in dispute and departments are being torn in half, the general project—which one shouldn't presume to describe exhaustively; it isn't that kind of thing—within which all the drama is happening is still in place.

The fact that it is in place does not mean that it is static and incapable of either entertaining or generating innovation. This, as we have seen, is another of Butler's complaints, that hewing to professional norms will block the emergence of new fields and new paradigms. But when new fields or paradigms emerge it is not because existing norms have been questioned from a perspective independent of them, but because existing norms have presided over their own alteration. When the profession extends itself by bringing into its orbit materials and avenues of inquiry it had previously ignored or excluded, the norms are not directly challenged and subjected to a searching critique; they are stretched. Let's say (to take one of Butler's examples) that women's studies has become part of the disciplinary landscape where previously it had no place. How did it happen? Well, at a certain point in the late sixties and early seventies the number of women in the profession increased dramatically. (In 1962 when I joined my first department it had over one hundred members only one of whom was a woman.) As female graduate students, alert to the women's movement, sat in the classes of their largely male teachers, they noticed something askew about the field of study they had entered— women writers were underrepresented in the curriculum, and those few women who made it into the canon were described and evaluated according to masculine models in the spirit of Hawthorne's famous complaint, in an 1855 letter to William Ticknor, against that "damned mob of scribbling women."

To notice something, however, is not simply to open up your eyes and see it; the eyes must be discipline-informed — informed, that is, by the norms that are now going to be altered by what they enable practitioners to notice. When you say that more women deserve to be in the canon, the standard of "deserving" is parasitic on the criteria for literariness that underwrite and constitute the field of literary studies. Those criteria — those norms — direct the effort to modify themselves (they are self-modifying), as you say, for example, that many women languishing in obscurity meet them or that they are too narrowly formulated and should be broadened. When that effort is successful (if it is; failure is always a possibility) and the disciplinary space no longer looks the same, the norms will still be in place even though the actions they set in motion and guide have somewhat transformed them. In her argument, Butler assumes the view of norms she attributes (wrongly, I think) to Post — that they are rigid and block change, whereas in fact they are engines of change.

Because the norms are engines of change and self-revision, they require no independent, outside effort to revise them. This is Butler's mistake, to believe that critique — standing back and surveying norms with the intention of deliberately interrogating them — is necessary for disciplinary change. The name for this mistake is "theory" — thinking that the warrants for the things we do reside far above the practical contexts in which we do them, reside, that is, in some very general proposition. The general/theoretical proposition Butler plumps for is that "norms are revisable in time" (123) or, in another version, that norms are *historically challengeable and socially negotiated* (120; emphasis in original). These are theoretical propositions because they pronounce in the abstract and have nothing to say about any particular, historically situated norm or the possible ways of revising it. They do no work. Saying that norms are revisable is not to have revised any or even to have begun the process. If you complain about the structure of exclusion that keeps your topics and concerns off the professional agenda, and, in response, someone says to you, "norms are revisable in time," you will not feel that you have received any help because a statement that general—that theoretical— doesn't direct you to any specific corrective action. The actions you might profitably be directed to would flow from your internalized understanding of the resources available to you in the very discipline whose boundaries you are pushing against, and your ability to move that discipline a millimeter or a mile would not depend on your believing or even knowing that norms are revisable in time.

The point, again, is that because academic norms (like any others) are underdetermined in their content and scope, the very act of applying them—of bringing them to bear on materials previously not part of the scene—will result in their alteration. No wholesale from-the-outside critique of the enterprise is required, nor, given the conservative nature of the academy, is likely to occur. Even the so-called theory revolution in literary studies unfolded in response to traditional questions about meaning, form, and value, and although theory gave new answers to those questions, the concerns that animated them—literary concerns—remained at the center. And that it is why when the theory boom was over, it was easy to return to familiar modes of inquiry, although, of course those modes, still identifiable in outline, had suffered a sea change by being washed in the waters of theory. Change does occur, not, however, as a willed principle—hey, let's change everything!—but as the consequence of working within the basic parameters of the practice. (Readers will recognize this as a Kuhnian perspective, a perspective that the sociologist Steve Fuller excoriates for its antidemocratic imperialist conservatism. In Thomas Kuhn's account of things, Fuller (2000) complains, "the natural spread of knowledge is captured by a community that gains relative advantage by forcing other communities to rely on its expertise" (37). That, of course, is professionalism's project.)

What defines a practice is not a set of theoretical propositions, but a firm understanding of its distinctiveness in the
Weinribian sense: it's a "this," not a "that." The practice will
remain what it is, even through many permutations, as long
it is still possible for practitioners to say "What we do is not
done by others who lack our training, and what others do we
don't pretend to do because we lack the expertise and it's not
our job." Butler's foregrounding of critique as the profession's
chief obligation and a key component of academic freedom
means that she is not committed to this distinctiveness and
is in fact suspicious of it, especially when it takes the form
of distinguishing between academic work and political work.
She finds a way of denying the distinction between academic
and political pronouncements by asserting a shared relationship to the public interest: "Although extramural expression
might not be exactly the same as academic expression, it would
seem that that they are nevertheless joined as two different
kinds of public interest" (Butler 2006a, 124). At a high level of
generality this is certainly true: both politics and the academy
are bound up in some way with the public interest. But this
shared characteristic should not obscure the fact, which Butler
acknowledges but doesn't take seriously, that the projects are
"two different kinds." The difference is key.

Butler attempts to blur the difference with a series of hypo-
theticals that actually tell against her point:

> If a historian of classical Greece starts to write on popular
> culture and reviews Michael Moore in a public venue or
> a Straussian political philosopher starts to write in the
> *Weekly Standard*, relating his political philosophy to
> contemporary foreign policy, the lines become somewhat
> blurred. (124)

No they don't. It depends on what kind of point the classicist
who reviews Michael Moore is making. Is he relating Moore's
documentaries to some general thesis about popular culture,
or is he affirming or rejecting Moore's partisan views? If it's
the former, he's still operating as an academic (although his

subject matter has changed) and his review is protected under the doctrine of academic freedom. If it's the latter, he has become a political agent and no academic freedom protection attaches. (And the venue doesn't matter; you can perform academically in the *Weekly Standard* as well as in the *Journal of English and German Philology*.) Butler is correct to say, on the basis of this and other examples, that the "professional profile of the scholar" often changes, but if the change is in the materials that are the object of analysis, the descriptive "scholar" is still accurate; if the change is in the mode of analysis, if the intention is to take partisan sides rather than to analyze a cultural artifact or event, "scholar" is no longer the title he or she can claim.

The distinction is further clarified by another example Butler employs: "An anthropologist who works in Kenya and Sudan may write essays on the genocide in Sudan and criticize his own country's policy, or a professor of constitutional law may write briefs regarding the legality of the war tribunals established for detainees at Camp Delta in Guantanamo." Butler imagines a tenure committee reviewing these materials and speculates that "reviewers would be hard pressed to distinguish between academic and extra-mural" (2006a, 124–25). No they wouldn't. The anthropologist who criticizes his own government is exercising the rights of a citizen, but he is not being an anthropologist (although he may be employing anthropological skills in the service of a political end) and what he writes in that mode should not be considered by the committee.

As for the professor of constitutional law, again it depends. Is he giving a professional analysis of the legality of the war tribunals or has he sold his expertise to an administration seeking justification for what it wants to do? If it is the second, his work can't count for academic credit, but neither can it count against him in academic contexts. Dean Christopher Edley Jr. of the University of California at Berkeley Law School was right to resist calls for the dismissal of law professor John Yoo, who had advised the George W. Bush administration that waterboarding and other "enhanced interrogation techniques" were not torture. Many academics disagreed vehemently with Yoo's judgment and conclusions and they were of course free to do so. What they were not free to do (although some did) was demand that he be deprived of his academic appointment because in a nonacademic context he elaborated and urged views which they despised.

The question finally is whether academic disciplines are mere placeholders for virtues and values that do not depend upon them for their definition and flourishing, or whether academic disciplines are constitutive of those virtues and values and so must be maintained in their integrity lest what they make possible be lost. (As we shall see, one of the things they make possible is a coherent rationale for academic freedom). That is the question debated in the second set of paired essays written by Post and Butler, and Post comes squarely down on the side of the constitutive force of disciplines. His authority is Alasdair MacIntyre (1981), who defines a practice (discipline) as "any coherent and complex form of socially established cooperative human activity through which goods internal to that form of activity are realized in the course of trying to achieve those standards of excellence which are appropriate to, and partially definitive of, that form of activity" (175). (Notice that it's "goods internal to that form of activity," not goods in the abstract.) MacIntyre acknowledges, as Post and I do, that the norms presiding over the practice "are not themselves immune from criticism," but he insists, as I would, that "nonetheless we cannot be initiated into a practice without accepting the authority of the best standards realized so far" (177). (Thomas Kuhn makes the same point in *The Structure of Scientific Revolutions*.)

To not accept that authority—to regard oneself as a free moral/political agent who just happens to sit in a university office—is to undermine, not improve, the basis on which professional projects can be undertaken and judgments of value made. Disciplinary scholarship cannot proceed by determinedly flouting or jettisoning the normative structures that give it shape. As Post (2009) writes, it cannot be "*inherently* 'subversive" or "intrinsically revolutionary" or "promiscuously unsettling" (760; emphasis in original). That is, it cannot be the job of disciplinary scholarship to subvert and unsettle the status quo, although, as I have already noted, the status quo will at once be maintained and reconfigured by successful disciplinary efforts. Endless critique may be the rallying cry of a political movement; it cannot be the rallying cry of academic work, for should it be so, the adjective "academic" would have no content of its own.

Once again, Butler (2009) disagrees. She begins by asking if "professional norms, construed in part as disciplinary norms, legitimate academic freedom, . . . what, if anything, legitimates such norms?" (776). In the event that the discipline's norms have judged an innovative "intellectual position" to be "rogue" and therefore "unspeakable," to what norms can one have recourse as a form of appeal or protest? Post would answer "to the very norms being challenged." He (2009) insists that a discipline's coherence depends on its mediating external challenges "through the filter of an established disciplinary culture" (769). Is this a recipe for conservatism? Butler (2009) certainly thinks so: *If disciplinary innovation becomes the price we pay in order to establish a basis on which to legitimate an argument against unwanted political intrusions, then it would seem we establish a conservative academic culture*" (794; emphasis in original). Well, yes and no. Yes, if you mean by "conservative culture," a culture slow to revise, never mind surrender, its understanding of what is and is not appropriate to it. As many have observed, because disciplines give the benefit of any doubt to established ways of doing things, they are inherently conservative.

And that, Judith Jarvis Thomson (1990) explains, is how it should be: "new fields, indeed, new ideas generally, have the burden of proof." Someone who offers a new idea or a new agenda is asking us, she says, to revise what we believe about what belongs in a discipline, and we in turn require him or her to provide "what we—given our past experience—can see to be reason to revise our beliefs" (160). The reason cannot have its source in some general right or obligation to perform critique; rather it must be a reason that those invested in the very norms under challenge can recognize; disciplinary reasons are the reasons that count when a disciplinary norm is being challenged. The appeal is not to some abstract and extradisciplinary standard of justice, but to the standards that underlie the enterprise and give it its shape. The question is not whether from the perspective of eternity or absolute truth there is reason to rethink things or stretch the boundaries, but whether from the perspective of the accumulated professional wisdom there is reason to rethink things or stretch the boundaries. "For what is in question is whether *we* would be acting responsibly in refusing to reverse ourselves—not whether an all-knowing God would, but whether we would" (160; emphasis in original).

Thomson is aware that this line of argument can be heard as an outright refusal "to welcome new ideas" and a determination to act as "defenders of an orthodoxy," but she insists that those proposing innovations will have gotten a fair hearing as long as we as insiders "have exercised the appropriate degree of care . . . and have made our assessment on scholarly grounds without excessive love of our own commitments" (163). (Notice that she doesn't counsel having *no* love for our commitments; that would be perverse.) The fact that in time the ideas and agendas we exclude may turn out to be fruitful beyond anything we had imagined and come to be honored by the very institution that once rejected them does not tell against our judgment; we are required, says Thomson, to be serious and responsible, not to be right. To be sure, the triumph of innovation, should it occur, will be slower than it would have been in the absence of disciplinary gatekeepers, but well-developed traditions of inquiry are justifiably slow to assess "unconventional . . . new ideas," for "replicating the work that issued in the new ideas, and then studying their further implications takes time"; and this is why, Thomson observes, "the scientist has to work at the enterprise of getting his or her new ideas accepted" (162, n. 8).

But acceptance is a possibility—it does happen—and therefore Butler's opposition between a conservative academic culture and an academic culture open to revision is a false one: Academic culture is both conservative, in that it quite rightly privileges established ways of doing business (they after all have earned their privilege), and open to revision, in that challenges to established protocols are always heard, although the bar to their succeeding is set very high. (David Downing [2005] criticizes this argument, which, he says, allows me complacently to situate myself on the left and the right at the same time: I acknowledge the conventional and revisable nature of academic norms, but, he complains, I declare them necessary in a gesture that ensures the maintenance of the discipline's gate-keeping mechanisms and of the status quo in general.)

It is this incrementalism, this limiting of critique to what the norms under pressure will recognize as a legitimate challenge, that Butler (2009) rejects in the name of strong critique. Taking her cue from Foucault (and with Derrida always in the background), she insists that "one has to be able to think beyond the domain of the thinkable that is established by . . . authority and on which that authority relies." To do that, she continues, is to "elaborate a position for oneself outside the ontological jurisdiction of that authority and so to elaborate a certain possibility of the subject" in which "one becomes, at the moment of being critical, irrational or nonrational, a rogue subject as it were, unintelligible within those political terms, and yet with a critical relationship to existing modes of intelligibility" (790).

The academy delivers a world complete with priorities, boundaries, legitimate and illegitimate activities, in short, norms. If one stays within those norms, Butler complains, the critique one can perform stops short of subjecting them to critical scrutiny. It is not enough, in her view, to point out and abide by the received-in-place distinctions between the legitimate and the illegitimate, the speakable and the unspeakable; one must inquire into how those distinctions came to be, or at least seem to be, perspicuous and obvious. The rogue subject, stepping as it were into another universe of discourse in which the conversation is not continued but brusquely changed, refuses the lure of intelligibility as it has been defined by the system, and goes boldly where institutional man or woman has been told not to go. This form of strong critique lays bare the devices through which weak critique—critique allowed by the system, but not extended to the system—puts a stop to itself. "The norms that establish the modes of intelligibility and recognizability for a subject are themselves queried, called into question, and so the very social basis for the intelligibility of the subject is risked at the moment in which such historical norms are interrogated" (788).

The risk (and reward) of being "rogue" is exemplified for Butler by debates "centered on the legitimacy of certain state authorities," debates those authorities work hard to foreclose by invoking the very authority under challenge; and she sees a parallel between such moments of political foreclosing and the foreclosing by the academy of inquiries into the legitimacy of its present structure of inclusions and exclusions. The two forms of foreclosure—the political and the academic—converge, she says, in the argument over whether Israel's treatment of the Palestinians is an appropriate topic of academic discussion:

> It makes sense that the debates about the legitimacy of the Israeli state . . . would form the center of debates on the proper purview of academic freedom. If academic freedom depends on critique, and critique is bound up with the question of how state legitimation takes place, then it would seem that the questions raised about Israel's subordination of the Palestinians prove to be a test case for whether or not critique can remain at the center of academic freedom at this time. (794–95)

The logic of this sequence depends on an equivocation in the "if" clause of the second sentence—"If academic freedom depends on critique. . . ." Academic freedom may be said to depend on critique in two quite different senses: either (1) the academic task of advancing knowledge necessarily involves a critical assessment of the received wisdom on the academic topic under consideration; or (2) what academics are free (and obligated) to do is critique existing arrangements whether or not they have traditionally been thought to fall within the academic "purview." Understood in the first sense, critique is directed only at matters in dispute in academic journals and conferences; what falls within the purview of academic consideration are the kinds of things that are taught in graduate school and are the basis of dissertations—the conventions of pastoral poetry, the causes of World War I, the competing philosophical accounts of truth. Understood in the second sense, critique extends into the wider world and brings back to the academy live political issues which are then debated as if the classroom were no different from a congressional hearing or a political rally. In this second sense of critique, there is no specifically academic form of critique; there is just critique which takes as its object anything it spots. In short, critique knows no boundaries and certainly not the boundary between academic matters and political matters.

Butler obviously understands critique in this second sense and rejects what is to her the parochialism of the first. She believes that critique should not confine itself to disciplinary matters like the interpretation of poems or the taxonomy of historical periods, but should apply itself first to the structural conditions that confine academic discussions to such matters, and then to the extra-academic forces that would impose and maintain those conditions. "The exercise of calling existing authorities into question, moves outside the university into the broader terrain of politics" (791). Questions about "Israel's subordination of the Palestinians" provide a test case because any labeling of those questions as "extra-academic" would, in Butler's view, signal an arbitrary and political limiting of what academics can freely interrogate and challenge:

If we cannot pose the question by what right and through what means a given state has achieved its status quo as legitimate, then we have already eroded the claim not only of critique but also of dissent, without which the process of legitimation cannot take place. (794)

In this sentence, "through what means" and "by what right" are treated as the same kinds of questions. They are not. "Through what means" is (or can be) an academic question; answering it involves a consideration of the history in the course of which legitimation was achieved; it does not involve a judgment as to whether the claimed legitimacy is really legitimate. But "by what right" demands such a judgment; it asks not for an account of the achievement of legitimacy, but for its justification—tell me by what right you wield the authority you claim. It is hard to see why academics are the appropriate persons to be addressing a state with this demand, unless academics are regarded as political creatures first and as professionals only incidentally. This is exactly how Butler (2009) regards them. In her analysis, there is no specifically academic freedom, just a free-floating freedom not limited to or confined within any institution, going everywhere, ignoring "do not enter" signs, jumping over all fences: "The operation of critique takes place not only in the identifiable domains of philosophy and within the walls of the university but every time and any time the question of what constitutes a legitimate government command or policy is raised" (780). "What I am calling critique . . . is . . . an ungrounded inquiry into the legitimacy of existing grounds" (786). Ungrounded, that is, in any institutional goals or protocols or limits, all of which, she is saying, are the appropriate objects of critique, not limitations on its scope.

As stirring as this vision is, it is the very antithesis of academic freedom as it is understood by both the "It's just a job" school and the "For the common good" school. Members of those schools will insist that academic freedom can exist only if the adjective "academic" is taken seriously, which means distinguishing sharply between academic forms of interrogation and forms of interrogation that are powerful and worthy, but belong elsewhere. Butler identifies critique with "open inquiry" (776), but in the academy, inquiry is not open (nor is it open elsewhere); it is circumscribed by the prevailing, in-force declarations of what is and is not an appropriate academic question. It is these declarations, or norms, that Butler would challenge by assuming the "rogue viewpoint," a viewpoint which, she acknowledges, cannot be "spoken without doing some damage to the idea of what is speakable" and unspeakable (777). It is damage the doing of which she views with equanimity, but to do it—to erase any distinction between what questions belong in the academy and what questions do not—would be to make the academy and any usable (because limited) notion of academic freedom disappear.

Note too that "rogue" may be too large a claim insofar as it suggests a form of action that is not shaped and inflected by some set of in-place norms and conventions. The "roguery" Butler urges is not an escape from the "speakable" (as she may think it is), but a swerve from one realm of the speakable—the academic realm—to another realm of the speakable—the political, or, more precisely, a swerve from one conventional practice to another. The romanticism of the word "rogue" may mislead Butler into thinking that she is recommending a form of action that is, in fact, available to no one—action that floats free of any and all institutional constraints. No, she is recommending that the constraints appropriate to, and defining of, the academy be replaced by the constraints (and imperatives) that belong properly to the realm of partisan politics, and of course I cannot follow her.

This is not to say that within the academically bounded space the issue of Israel's behavior toward the Palestinians cannot be raised. It is perfectly OK to raise it as long as the point is to describe and analyze the conflict, not to take sides on it. Of course one could properly take sides on the question of whether the arguments put forward by either party are intellectually coherent; but it would be possible to decide, on the basis of academic criteria, that one party's arguments were better formulated and thought through, and still decide, on the basis of nonacademic criteria, that when all is said and done, the party with the less intellectually impressive arguments is in the right.

Classroom judgments are just that—judgments appropriate to the classroom—and they don't translate into judgments on real-world choices; they are limited. Butler, however, wants to go the whole way in the classroom; she wants issues not just to be anatomized, but to be fought out. And she thinks that academic freedom, properly understood, not only allows the blurring of the line between the academy and real-world politics, but requires it. In this logic, any move to cabin critique by, for example, keeping the question of Israel's legitimacy off the table as a question to be pronounced on (rather than analyzed) in the classroom, would constitute a diminishing of academic freedom. But (as I have been arguing), a diminished—not overly ambitious—concept of academic freedom is precisely what is required if academic freedom is to mean something as opposed to meaning everything. Academic freedom understood as a discipline-based concept, as a professional concept, cannot survive immersion in a sea of critique.

It is an irony (to say the least) that in her eagerness to take the "academic" out of academic freedom, Butler makes common cause with the figure who occupies the position of archvillain in several of her essays—David Horowitz. Horowitz is the founder of Students for Academic Freedom, author of the Academic Bill of Rights, and a champion of what he calls "intellectual diversity." Implementing intellectual diversity would require that departments (a) actively recruit faculty members who self-identify as political conservatives and (b) take care that course reading lists display an ideological balance. The reasoning is that an unbalanced faculty teaching an unbalanced curriculum will deliver knowledge in a politically biased way and thereby shortchange students. (The headnote on the Students for Academic Freedom website reads "You can't get a good education if they're only telling you half the story.") That reasoning informs the conclusion reached by Daniel B. Klein and Andrew Western (2005) when they surveyed departments at Stanford and UC Berkeley and found that Republicans are outnumbered nine to one.

To which my response is, "So what?" Although equal representation might be a principle of democracy, it cannot be a principle of the academy, if only because the business of the academy is to sort the wheat from the chaff and discard, not represent, points of view it judges unworthy; it does not give points of view a place at the table simply because someone out there is asserting them. Moreover, nothing can be fairly concluded about either the quality or direction of teaching from a survey of party affiliations. A faculty member's judgment as to which approach to a topic is fruitful, and the same faculty member's judgment as to which policies and politicians deserve his vote, are independent variables. The positions taken by individual teachers on disputed academic matters—qualitative versus quantitative social science, top-down history versus history from below, intentionalist constitutional interpretation versus textualist constitutional interpretation—do not track their partisan political persuasions. Requiring intellectual diversity—understood as the demand for proportionate political representation—will do nothing to improve the educational experience; but it will mandate the presence of certain partisan perspectives in the classroom.

In short, intellectual diversity is finally nothing more than a program of affirmative action for conservatives. There is nothing intellectual about it. It is a political not a pedagogical requirement, designed to ensure that students hear conservative voices, independently of whether an academic discipline has determined by disciplinary standards that those are the voices a student ought to hear. (It is if an athletic team were to sign players on the basis of their performance in the voting booth rather than on the basis of their performance on the field.) To the extent that students have a right of academic freedom, it is the right to be introduced to ideas and projects that have earned the academy's seal of approval (no Holocaust denial please), not the right to be introduced to a balanced array of political views.

Needless to say, the politics Horowitz would bring into the classroom is quite different from Butler's politics, but the two are allied in substituting for the imperatives of a narrow professionalism the imperatives of a political vision. Their respective visions are distinct—a left-leaning universalist critique versus the assertion and protection of conservative values—but neither is an academic vision, unless the word "academic" has been stretched to the point where it has no meaning of its own.

ACADEMIC EXCEPTIONALISM AND PUBLIC EMPLOYEE LAW

I shall return in a later chapter to the odd prominence of the Israeli-Palestinian conflict in debates about academic freedom, but for the moment I want to point out what should already be clear—that an expanded notion of critique (à la Butler), the idea of academic exceptionalism, and the location of academic freedom in the individual rather than in the institution, go together.

If academic freedom is assigned to the college or university, the scope of the individual faculty member's freedom is limited first by the norms embodied in the particular institution's regulations, and ultimately by the norms that are said, by tradition and disciplinary authority, to define the academic enterprise in general. If, however, academic freedom attaches to the individual, it is her sense (rather than any institutional sense) of what marks the proper boundaries of her activities that trumps. The way is then open, as Matthew Finkin and Robert Post (2009) observe, to decide "that academic freedom exists to protect the distinct value of free and critical inquiry" (43), where "free" does not mean "free within the constraints implicit in the institution's practices," but just "free"; and where "critical inquiry" does not mean "analytical inquiry," but debunking, deconstructive critique; and where "distinct" means "stand alone," that is, not defined by the goals and history of the setting that just happens to be its (temporary) habitation. Those who perform this activity owe their capacity for critique and their license to follow it wherever it goes not to their professional qualifications (although they might come in handy), but to an inner propensity to virtue and a passion for justice that justify the refusal to adhere to the institution's ordinary protocols. They are exceptional.

Urofsky v. Gilmore

The logic of exceptionalism is given a full expression in *Urofsky v. Gilmore* (Fourth Circuit, 2000), where it is rejected by the court. The case is exemplary for my purposes because it presents in sharp contrast two characterizations of academics who teach at public universities. In one characterization, university teachers are public employees no less bound by generally applicable laws and regulations than a clerk or custodian or assistant district attorney. In the other, university teachers, because they are engaged in the special activity of advancing knowledge, "deserve more freedom from employment control than typical employees" (King 2002, 354). In the course of debating these opposing views of the status of teachers in public universities, the judges of the Fourth Circuit revisited, without explicitly referencing, the 1915 American Association of University Professors' Declaration of Principles' comparison of university professors to judges: "University teachers should be understood to be, with respect to the conclusions reached and expressed by them, no more subject to the control of the trustees, than are judges subject to the control of the President" who appoints them. In both cases, the employer buys an independent judgment, not a judgment tailored to the employer's inclinations. *Urofsky v. Gilmore* explores the question of just how far this independence—we may call it academic freedom—goes.

The facts of the case (which I rehearsed briefly earlier) are as follows. In 1996 the legislature of the state of Virginia enacted Sections 21-804 to 806 of the Restrictions on State

Employee Access to Information Infrastructure Act. The relevant portion reads:

> Except to the extent required in conjunction with a bona fide agency-approved research project or other agency-approved undertaking, no agency employee shall utilize agency-owned or agency-leased computer equipment to access, download, print or store any information, infrastructure files or services having sexually explicit content. Such agency approval shall be given in writing by agency heads, and any such approval shall be available to the public under the provisions of the Virginia Freedom of Information Act.

In short, if you are a government employee and you want to access pornography on a state-owned computer, you have to get a waiver from a supervisor. Six faculty members in the university system filed a lawsuit arguing that the law was both overbroad (it swept up too much in its ambit) and underinclusive (it said nothing about other forms of disruptive behavior) with respect to all public employees, and in violation of the academic freedom rights of public employees who were professors. As Judge William Wilkins, writing for the majority, explained, the professors made a double argument; first that the rights of all state employees were infringed by the act, and, second, that even if the act is constitutional when applied to ordinary employees, it is unconstitutional when applied to professors. "Appellees maintain that even if the Act is valid as to the majority of state employees, it violates the First Amendment academic freedom rights of professors, . . . and thus is invalid as to them" (*Urofsky v. Gilmore*, 216 F.3d 401, 409).

There is a weak way and a strong way to read appellees' claim. Are they saying that unlike file clerks and mail carriers, academics do work that sometimes requires accessing "sexually explicit content," and this difference should be taken into account (as it is by the waiver mechanism); or are they saying that even the slightest state interference with a professor's freedom to follow his or her research/teaching inclinations is an impermissible infringement on academic freedom? Judge Wilkins is certain that it is the second: "In essence, Appellees contend that a university professor possesses a constitutional right to determine for himself, without the input of the university (and perhaps even contrary to the university's desires) the subjects of his research, writing, and teaching" (*Urofsky v. Gilmore*, 216 F.3d 401, 410).

Wilkins perfectly articulates the strong claim for academic freedom that follows from the doctrine of academic exceptionalism, and he immediately denies it. "Our review of the law, however, leads us to conclude that to the extent the Constitution recognizes any right of 'academic freedom' above and beyond the First Amendment rights to which every citizen is entitled, the right inheres in the University, not in individual professors, and is not violated by the terms of the Act" (*Id.* at 410). Doubtful that academic freedom has any constitutional status, Wilkins is sure that no such status attaches to the labors of individual professors, who must rest their case not on an asserted academic freedom right, but on the First Amendment rights any public employee possesses.

What are those rights? It has been generally recognized that a citizen's full First Amendment freedom can be somewhat curtailed (although not abrogated) by the conditions and requirements of his or her employment. A nurse who made a plea for higher salaries in the middle of an operation could not successfully invoke the First Amendment if she were disciplined or dismissed. When the employer is the government, the situation is somewhat complicated because, in general, the citizen's First Amendment rights are rights against government interference with his or her free expression. In the role of employer, however, the government has the same ability to regulate disruptive expression as might be claimed by any other employer concerned with the good order and efficiency of the workplace. Paradoxical as it might seem, the government has a greater scope for discipline and punishment in the limited role of employer than it has in the larger role of sovereign. "Content-based restrictions on speech are problematic vis-à-vis the public but may be appropriate when the sovereign acts as a public employer" (Tepper and White 2009, 148).

Justice Thurgood Marshall made the relevant point in *Pickering v. Board of Education* (1968), a leading case. Although public school teachers cannot be required to "relinquish [their] First Amendment rights" as the price for public employment, "it cannot be gainsaid that the State has interests as an employer that differ significantly from those it possesses in connection with regulation of the speech of the citizenry in general." The task, Marshall continued, "is to arrive at a balance between the interests of the teacher as a citizen in commenting on matters of public concern, and the interest of the State, as an employer, in promoting the efficiency of the public services it performs through its employees" (*Pickering v. Bd. of Ed. of Twp. High Sch. Dist. 205, Will County, Illinois*, 391 U.S. 563, 568).

In the cases that followed Pickering, the phrase "matters of public concern," which as we shall see, is a term of art rather than a common-sense category, became the key to defining the appropriate balance. In *Connick v. Myers* (1983), Justice Byron White articulated the standard: "When employee expression cannot be fairly considered as relating to any matter of political, social, or other concern to the community, government officials should enjoy wide latitude in managing their offices without intrusive oversight by the judiciary in the name of the First Amendment" (*Connick v. Myers*, 461 U.S. 138, 146). The first step then is to determine whether the speech at issue relates to a matter of public concern. If it doesn't, the government as employer can regulate and/or penalize it. If it does, the court will then weigh the speaker's First Amendment interests against the government-as-employer's interest in managing its workplace. The thumb on the scale favors the employer; the employee must jump two hurdles before he can prevail on the assertion of his rights. And that is as it should be, says Justice White, for "to presume that all matters which transpire within a government office are of public concern would mean that virtually every remark—and certainly every criticism directed at a public office—would plant the seed of a constitutional case" (*Id.* at 149). "Government offices," he adds "could not function if every employment decision became a constitutional matter" (*Id.* at 143).

When the Pickering-Connick test is applied, a line must be drawn between what is and is not a matter of public concern (as legally defined), and that has not always been easy to do. (One commentator complains that "the difficulties in developing any principled approach to the public concern test render it essentially standardless" [Rosenthal 1998, 551n114].) Justice White makes an effort to draw the line when he announces the Court's holding in *Connick*:

> We hold . . . that when a public employee speaks not as a citizen upon matters of public concern, but instead as an employee upon matters of personal interest . . . a federal court is not the appropriate forum in which to review the wisdom of a personnel decision taken by a public agency allegedly in reaction to the employee's behavior. (*Connick v. Myers*, 461 U.S. 138, 147)

(In short, we decide cases, not interoffice squabbles.)

Sheila Myers, an assistant district attorney in New Orleans, was upset when she was transferred to a new assignment within the district attorney's office. Her protests were unavailing and she took it upon herself to prepare and distribute a questionnaire "soliciting the views of her fellow staff members concerning office transfer, office morale," and other matters (*Connick v. Myers* 461 U.S. 138, 147). Her superiors considered her behavior disruptive and she was terminated. She then filed a suit on First Amendment grounds and lost because the Court decided that hers was a personal grievance, of interest to her, to be sure, but not of interest to the public. (The relevance of this line of cases to the issue of academic freedom may not yet be clear, but, trust me, it soon will be.)

One of Myers's questions, Justice White acknowledges, did "touch upon a matter of public concern"; it asked whether assistant district attorneys "ever feel pressured to work in political campaigns on behalf of office supported candidates" (*Connick v. Myers*, 461 U.S. 138, 149). Here then is a clear distinction between Myers speaking as a citizen to other citizens who might be concerned with corruption in a public agency, and Myers as a disgruntled employee who is using a questionnaire to express her displeasure at having been transferred. Applying the balancing test with respect to that one question, the Court decides that because "Myers's questionnaire touched upon matters of public concern only in a most limited sense," the employer wins the day: "When employee speech concerning office policy arises from an employment dispute concerning the very application of that policy to the speaker, additional weight must be given to the supervisor's view that the employee has threatened the authority of the employer to run the office" (*Id.* at 153).

Urofsky v. Gilmore stands for the proposition that this holds true even if the employee is a professor. Judge Wilkins follows the Pickering-Connick line of reasoning faithfully and finds that public employees who seek to access explicitly sexual materials on state-owned computers are not speaking as citizens about matters of public concern, but expressing a personal wish to have the workplace configured in a way that pleases them. "Because . . . the challenged aspect of the Act does not affect speech by Appellees in their capacity as private citizens speaking on matters of public concern, it does not infringe the First Amendment rights of state employees." The threshold for invoking the Pickering-Connick test had not been reached and therefore no balancing test is required (*Urofsky v. Gilmore*, 216 F.3d 401, 409).

That would have been the end of it were it not for the appellees' second claim, that because they are professors, an obligation that would legitimately bind others does not bind them. As we have seen, Wilkins makes short work of this argument. "Because the Act does not infringe the constitutional rights of employees in general, it does not violate the rights of professors." That is, there is only one category to be considered—public employees; being a professor affords you no additional suit of constitutional armor (*Urofsky v. Gilmore*, 216 F.3d 401, 415).

In a concurring opinion, Judge J. Michael Luttig is even more blunt. Noting that the appellees assert "a First Amendment right of 'academic freedom'" that "is reserved for professors alone," he reaffirms the Pickering-Connick doctrine: "When university professors conduct university research on university time, on university computers, and in conduct of their university duties, it is indisputable that they are performing in their roles as public employees" and not as citizens (*Urofsky v. Gilmore*, 216 F.3d 401, 417, 421 [Luttig, J., concurring]). And as for the argument "that the public university's professors operate independently of state supervision," Luttig scorns it, saying "it is a surprise to me, and I am confident that it would come as a surprise to the public who pays the professors' salaries in order that they may conduct important research for the public and without whose tax support the professors' research and writing would not be possible" (*Id.* at 424). Luttig explicitly rejects the exceptionalist premise in the appellees' arguments. He sees no reason to believe "that the academy has a special contribution to make to society beyond that that the ordinary citizen is able to make" or "that its 'speech' should enjoy constitutional protection that other employees' speech should not" (*Id.* at 417).

There is a dissent and a concurrence that reads like a dissent. Chief Judge J. Harvie Wilkinson III agrees with his colleagues in the majority that the state has pursued "a legitimate interest through minimally intrusive means," i.e., by permitting university officials to grant waivers for all bona fide research projects. In their brief the appellees assert that scholars should not be "required to obtain a license" for "studying all that might be 'lascivious'"; but all that is required is that they demonstrate that studying, and not something else, is what they are doing. Therefore, Wilkinson concludes, the act is constitutional (*Urofsky v. Gilmore*, 216 F.3d 401, 426 [Wilkinson, J., concurring]).

He objects, however, to his colleagues' reliance on the citizen/employee distinction. By making the distinction the "dispositive criterion, the majority rests its conclusion solely on the 'form' of the speech" and neglects, he charges, to inquire into its content (*Urofsky v. Gilmore*, 216 F.3d 401, 427). Although the plaintiff professors may not be speaking directly to citizens about matters currently before the public, the content of the topics they address in their research "surely touches on matters of political and social importance," and their wisdom should not be withheld from the public just because some policy internal to an institution's operation places restrictions on employee speech (*Id.* at 427). "One cannot possibly contend," Wilkinson declares, "that research in socially useful subjects such as medicine, biology, anatomy, sociology, anthropology, law, economics, art history, literature, and philosophy is not a matter of public concern" (*Id.* at 428).

The distinction between form (the role a speaker occupies as either citizen or employee) and content (the substance of what she says) with respect to the "matters of public concern" test tracks the distinction I have been explicating between academic freedom as a limited, guild concept—a matter of what academics as trained and salaried professionals should and shouldn't do—and academic freedom as a general obligation, shared by but not limited to academics, to perform as the guardians and watchdogs of truth. Are academics responsible to the norms of the profession, or do they have a higher and exceptional responsibility to serve as society's whistleblowers? Wilkinson opts for the second prong when he insists that the court should look not to the role of the professor (the formal institutional conditions of her utterance) in order to determine the protection she deserves, but to the importance to society (the content) of what she has to say. Her location in a university setting, with its narrowly framed obligations and restrictions, is not the central thing; she may just as well have been broadcasting her views on a street corner. The central thing is whether she is saying something the public might be interested in hearing, and as Wilkinson's list of the "socially useful subjects" academics study indicates, it would be hard in his view for anything a professor says not to fall into that category.

In Wilkinson's argument, then, professorial speech and matters of public concern are for all intents and purposes one and the same. Professors, he declares, "are hired for the very purpose of inquiring into, reflecting upon, and speaking out on matters of public concern" (*Urofsky v. Gilmore*, 216 F.3d 401, 428 [Wilkinson, J., concurring]). (This might come as a surprise to the appointment committee charged to come up with the scholar most qualified to teach medieval history or the nineteenth-century lyric.) Because the job of professors is to pronounce on matters "touching our physical health, our mental well-being, our economic prosperity, and ultimately our appreciation for the world around us," the public has an interest and investment in everything they do (*Id.* at 428).

Matthew Finkin (1988), a noted scholar of academic freedom, makes the same point: "there is little that occurs on the campus that is not of 'political,' 'social,' or at least 'other' concern to the larger community" (1346). If the test is whether an utterance touches on issues that have "broad social impact"—Wilkinson's test—all academic utterances pass it by definition and are thereby worthy of protection even if the same degree of protection is denied to the custodians and secretaries who labor in the same workplace. This, of course, is precisely the position of the appellees in *Urofsky* and amounts to a textbook definition of academic exceptionalism. (This elevation of academic discourse to a general matter of public concern lives on in the law. In *Demers v. Austin* [2013], Judge William Fletcher of the U.S. Court of Appeals for the Ninth Circuit declares that although it may seem "trivial" to some, the debate in English departments about the literary canon is a matter of "importance to our culture" [*Demers v. Austin*, No. 11–35558].)

In his dissent, Judge Francis D. Murnaghan Jr. brings Wilkinson's general point home to the speech at issue. The appellees in *Urofsky*, he says, "easily" meet the "matter-of-public-concern" test because everyone is interested in sex. "The Supreme Court has stated that 'sex, a great and mysterious motive force in human life, has indisputably been a subject of absorbing interest to mankind through the ages; it is one of the vital problems of human interest and public concern'" (*Urofsky v. Gilmore*, 216 F.3d 401, 438). (The quotation is from the 1957 case *Roth v. United States*, perhaps not the best citation given that *Roth* affirms the power of Congress to ban the publication of materials the average person might find obscene [*Roth v. United States*, 354 U.S. 476, 487].) Here then is the syllogism: speech related to matters of public concern merits First Amendment protection; the public is always interested in sex; therefore public employees who use state-owned computers to access sexually explicit materials are engaging in protected speech, especially if they are academics.

As is often the case, the syllogism falters in its middle proposition: to say that everyone is always interested in sex is one thing; to say that sex is a matter of public concern is another. "Interest" is a statistical measure; "matter of public concern" is a legal term of art. To be sure, there are contexts—sexual liaisons between a teacher and his pupils, police officers who sexually assault witnesses or suspects, politicians who use campaign funds to finance extramarital affairs—in which sex is a matter of public concern in the legally relevant sense: something the public should know about as it goes about the business of electing leaders and voting on policies. But the more general sense of "public concern," which is equivalent to "whatever members of the public might be interested in," cannot be asserted as a *legal* reason unless the concern in question can be related either to matters currently before the public or to matters the public has a right to know about. The public is generally interested in sports, but that doesn't mean that public employees have a constitutional right to talk sports in the workplace. Ditto with sex.

Wilkinson's and Murnaghan's argument rests on an equivocation between "matters of public concern" as a concept denoting matters pertinent to policy decisions and "matters of public concern" as a category so capacious that it includes everything. (And, as I have already said, this is very much like the equivocation between academic freedom as a concept tied to the performance of the limited academic job and academic freedom as a license for professors to say and do whatever they like, subject only to the restriction that they do so in the service of a great cause.) It is an equivocation the Fourth Circuit had already rejected in an earlier case:

> Because almost anything that occurs within a public agency could be of concern to the public, we do not focus on the inherent interest of the matters discussed by the employee. Rather our task is to decide whether the speech at issue in a particular case was made primarily in the plaintiff's role as citizen or primarily in his role as employee. In making this determination, the mere fact that the topic of the employee's speech was one in which the public might or would have had a great interest is of little moment. (*DiMeglio v. Haines*, 45 F.3d 790 [4th Cir. 1995])

In short, it is not the content of the speech—its "inherent interest"—that determines the level of protection, but the role (citizen or employee) the speaker presently inhabits. Honoring the distinction between form and content and insisting on the priority of form—of the formal, institutional identity of the speaker—is essential if "matter of public concern" is to be a reasonably cabined concept and not a free pass for anything a professor thinks to say.

In the academic community *Urofsky v. Gilmore* has been received with dismay and characterized by one commentator as a decision that "has desiccated legal protection for professors' academic freedom" (Rendleman 2002, 369). The same commentator explains why, in his view, professors need and deserve more latitude than do other citizens. Because "good professors possess critical intelligence" and are employed "to test the prevailing wisdom," the government "should protect a professor's scholarly speech more than an ordinary employee's speech" (364). That is to say, there is a special class of wise persons whose job it is to monitor the thought and speech of the rest of us; accordingly, when they speak the usual rules don't apply. There's the formula: mix equal parts of exceptionalism and critique, and lo and behold, you have an academic freedom that floats free of any constraints, professional or legal.

But of course that's not the way *Urofsky* was decided. As Alison Paige Landry (2001), then assistant attorney general of Virginia, observed, *Urofsky* "reaffirms that the First Amendment is not *carte blanche* for 'those who know better,' including faculty" (25). The case, Landry continued, "teaches that academic freedom is not synonymous with a right to eschew institutional oversight. Regardless of the contractual insularities of tenure, under the First Amendment no professor is a sovereign unto him or herself . . . when his professional agenda conflicts with his employer's" (24). Landry builds on a point made by Judge Wilkins in passing: "academic freedom [is] a professional norm, not a legal one" (*Urofsky v. Gilmore,* 216 F.3d 401, 411). That is to say, despite the many references to academic freedom in the courts and in the law reviews, academic freedom, as I suggested in the introduction to this book, has no substantial presence in the law. It is perfectly reasonable for academics, like any other group of workers, to desire working conditions that afford maximum freedom of action, but the realization of that desire is a matter of contract or disciplinary convention, not of law or constitutional right.

That is *Urofsky*'s lesson. Win your rights at the bargaining table or in the academic senate, not in the abstract realm of constitutional law. It is a lesson, Landry knows, that many academics will resist: "To the extent that some academics really do believe that professors have 'more' constitutional rights than other employees, *Urofsky.* . . dramatically rejects that view, taking pains to level the playing field of free expression between professors and custodians" (26).

Garcetti v. Ceballos
Leveling the playing field, as *Urofsky* arguably does, redresses the imbalance that occurs when professors act, or attempt to

act, as if the constraints placed on "ordinary" workers do not apply to them. But there is an argument to be made that *Urofsky* goes too far by failing to recognize that while academics do not stand outside the usual categories of public employment, they are different in a way that lawmakers should take into account. All too often, J. Peter Byrne (1989) declares, "courts fail to recognize that universities are fundamentally different from business corporations, government agencies and churches" and that "universities require legal provisions tailored to their own goals and problems" (254). Again, the relevant distinction is between "different" (an empirical measure) and "special" (a moral measure). In the context of this distinction, there is no contradiction in contending on the one hand that academics are not special in the sense of being exceptional, and on the other that the task academics are assigned (the advancement of truth) is sufficiently unlike other tasks to require for its successful performance a degree of freedom from monitoring not accorded to nonacademics.

The difficulty that ensues if one makes no distinction at all between academics and other public employees is an explicit topic in *Garcetti v. Ceballos* (2006). Richard Ceballos, in his capacity as a calendar deputy in the office of the district attorney of Los Angeles, determined that an affidavit used in a search warrant was inaccurate. Accordingly he drafted a memo recommending dismissal of the case. After a heated meeting, his supervisors decided to proceed with the prosecution. Ceballos stood by his conclusions, arguing, among other things, that he felt obligated to share his internal memorandum with the defense. In the months following, he was denied a promotion and reassigned. In response he sued, "alleging retaliation for his . . . memo, in violation of the First and Fourteenth Amendments" (*Garcetti v. Ceballos*, 547 U.S. 410).

The Supreme Court, with Justice Anthony Kennedy writing for the majority, ruled that because the memo was written "pursuant to his employment duties," Ceballos's speech was not protected. "Restricting speech that owes its existence to a public employee's professional responsibilities does not infringe any liberties the employee might have enjoyed as a private citizen" (*Garcetti v. Ceballos*, 547 U.S. 410, 421). The government as employer has commissioned the speech produced in the course of regular duties and may react to it as it sees fit. "If Ceballos' superiors thought his memo was inflammatory or misguided, they had the authority to take proper corrective action" (*Id.* at 423). The ruling, Kennedy concludes, "simply reflects the exercise of employer control over what the employer itself has commissioned or created." Therefore "we reject . . . the notion that the First Amendment shields from discipline the expressions employees make pursuant to their professional duties." It can't be the case that there is a "constitutional cause of action behind every statement a public employee makes in the course of doing his or her job" (*Id.* at 425).

As Lara Geer Farley (2007) points out, the majority opinion in *Garcetti* creates a barrier to an employee's invocation of the Pickering-Connick test: even if the speech at issue is arguably a matter of public concern, should that speech have been produced "pursuant to . . . public duties," it will be "beyond the protection of the First Amendment" (605). "When a public employee makes a statement pursuant to his official duties, he is not speaking as a citizen for First Amendment purposes, and the Constitution will not insulate his communication from employer discipline" (614).

In a brief dissent, Justice John Paul Stevens challenges the "pursuant to official duties" test and the citizen/employee distinction on which it rests: "The notion that there is a categorical difference between speaking as a citizen and speaking in the course of one's employment is quite wrong" (*Garcetti v. Ceballos*, 547 U.S. 410, 427 [Stevens, J., dissenting]). The question of constitutional protection, he declares, should not turn on whether the speech at issue was uttered while the speaker was on the job. Citing an earlier case in which the court affirmed an English teacher's First Amendment rights when she complained to the principal about racist employment practices, he insists that "it is senseless to let constitutional protection for exactly the same words hinge on whether they fall within a job description" (*Id.* at 427). Or, in other words, look to the content, not to the form.

In a lengthier dissent, Justice David Souter goes in another direction. Rather than dismissing form or role as a basis for determining levels of protection, he retains the citizen/employee distinction, but complicates it by further distinguishing between two classes of employees—those who are hired to "'promote a particular policy' by broadcasting a message set by the government" and those who are expected to exercise independent judgment in the context of a general responsibility like the responsibility "to enforce the law by constitutional action" (*Garcetti v. Ceballos*, 547 U.S. 410, 437 [Souter, J., dissenting]). Souter argues that Ceballos falls within the second class (a question that need not concern us here), and, to illustrate the danger of having a blanket rule that applies without distinction to all public employees, he points to those public employees who are academics: "I have to hope that today's majority does not mean to imperil First Amendment protection of academic freedom in public colleges and universities, whose teachers necessarily speak and write 'pursuant to official duties'" (*Id.* at 438). (Justice Kennedy responds by saying that the question of academic employees has not been addressed.)

The merit of Souter's argument for our purposes is that it at once preserves the distinction between speaking as a citizen and speaking as an employee and points the way to affording academics a superior measure of protection without placing them in an entirely special category. Academics, it could be said, belong in both of Souter's employee categories: in some instances, their speech is commissioned and supervised by the government as employer, but in other instances their speech breaks free of employer direction, albeit in ways the employer approves and even desires.

Suppose, for example, you are a professor of history and you are teaching a section of a required course in U.S. history. Are you free to substitute for the assigned textbook one of your choice? Can you be disciplined if you do? No, to the first question and yes to the second. The choice of textbook in a multisection course belongs to the administration. Striking out in your own direction is not an admirable exercise of creative independence; it is insubordination.

But now suppose you publish a scholarly essay in which you question the usefulness of required courses, criticize the textbook you were obligated to use, and argue that the themes that structure the standard course in U.S. history, including the course offered by your own department, are the wrong ones. Is the writing of that essay an act of insubordination? Can you be disciplined for it? Might you be rewarded for it? No to the first two questions, yes to question three. Although as an academic some of the speech you produce is "commissioned and created" by your employer, who has the right to monitor and assess your performance, with respect to some other forms of speech required by your official duties, your commission is not to be faithful to authority and settled wisdom but to go beyond them.

The point is that unlike an assistant district attorney, a college or university professor is hired to perform two different (but related) set of duties. On the one hand, his speech must conform to certain guidelines; he can't depart from the stipulated subject matter and start talking about his marriage or his finances, and he can't announce to his class on U.S. history that for the rest of the semester we will be discussing the evils of processed foods. But on the other hand, when he embarks on a research project, the present boundaries of the subject are not to be respected but challenged; he is still beholden to his employer, but what the employer has "bought" is a set of skills, not a particular conclusion to which they must be bent. Erica Goldberg and Kelly Sarabyn (2011) explicate the distinction: "The most sensible way to protect the academic freedom rights of faculty at public institutions is to treat them as akin to independent contractors on the issue of speech—their speech is funded, but not directed or scripted, by the government" (252).

Thus Robert O'Neil (2008) doesn't have it quite right when he asserts that "the clarity with which a court can determine the responsibilities of an assistant attorney . . . simply does not apply to assistant professors" (18). Yes it does, as long as it is recognized that the assistant professor has different responsibilities depending on whether he is in the classroom (and on what kind of class it is, a survey or a seminar) or in the archive, and that his different roles have attached to them different degrees of freedom and constraint and different degrees of protection. If he is doing one job—carrying out the directives of the institution—his speech is company property in the *Garcetti* sense and is subject to criticism and discipline. If he is doing another job—boldly going where no other scholar has gone before—the company has authorized him to depart from the zone of its control. He is still producing speech pursuant to his duties, but his duty is not defined by his employer's desire for a particular outcome; and whatever outcome he achieves cannot be the occasion of rebuke or penalty simply because his employer doesn't like it. (Although, of course, his speech may be penalized if his employer—a dean or a provost—finds it not up to the university's academic standards.)

Robert J. Tepper and Craig G. White (2009) survey the post-*Garcetti* landscape and conclude that universities do in fact recognize this difference in their practice: "While most universities require faculty members to pursue research and scholarship, they do not regulate the creative process and often do not claim ownership of the work" (171). Judith Areen (2009) explains this double perspective by invoking a distinction between the government-as-employer and government-as-educator. "In a government-as-educator case, a faculty member first would have to show that his or her expression met the academic matter test—that is, that the speech was concerned with research, teaching or academic governance matters." Should the faculty expression fail "to meet this burden, then the jurisprudence of government-as-employer should be followed" (987). In other words, if what is at issue touches core academic concerns, First Amendment and academic freedom rights are implicated, but if the issues are on the periphery of the core academic enterprise, the Pickering-Connick-Garcetti line of cases rules.

David Rabban (1990) makes a similar argument when he uses the touchstone of "critical inquiry" to draw the line separating protected speech from speech that can be regulated without violating academic freedom: "Disagreements over curricular and other educational policy issues seem sufficiently linked to critical inquiry to come within the specific theory of academic freedom. Disputes over salary or offices do not" (295). Paul Horwitz (2007) describes the proper balance in a particularly crisp formulation: "Universities are not entitled to blanket immunity from the general operation of the law but they should be entitled to a substantial deference . . . to the extent that they are making genuinely academic decisions" (1541). Each of these commentators marks the relevant distinction in his or her favorite terms, but they all make the same common sense point: academic work is in fact different, and both policy and law should take that difference into account. That difference, however, does not extend to everything in the workplace situation, and in many respects academics are employees like anyone else.

Intramural Criticism

Properly interpreted, then, the *Garcetti* holding poses no threat to academic freedom, modestly conceived as the freedom to do the academic job. But it does have distressing implications for those who believe that at the heart of academic freedom is the freedom to criticize one's superiors without fear of reprisal. This is called the freedom of intramural criticism and its exercise has been denied protection in a number of post-*Garcetti* decisions.

In *Gorum v. Sessoms* (2008), Professor Wendell Gorum contended that his dismissal from Delaware State College, ostensibly because he had altered grades in violation of university policy, was actually an act of retaliation by a president who objected to his speech on three occasions: when he "voiced opposition to the finalists during the presidential selection process"; when he revoked an invitation extended to the president to speak at a breakfast; and when he provided advice and assistance to a student facing suspension. The court held that Gorum "spoke as a public employee pursuant to his official duties" and that "the Constitution does not insulate this kind of speech and provide Gorum the protection he seeks." In short, he was in each instance performing a task pursuant to his duties, and the administration had the right and authority to evaluate and, perhaps, penalize his performance if it saw fit to do so (*Gorum v. Sessoms*, C.A.06–565 [(GMS], 2008 WL 399641 [D. Del. Feb. 12, 2008] *aff'd*, 561 F.3d 179 [3d Cir. 2009]).

In *Renken v. Gregory* (2008), Professor Kevin Renken contended that his pay was reduced and a National Science Foundation grant terminated in retaliation for his having criticized the administration's position on a number of issues related to the use of grant funds. Among other things, Renken stated in an e-mail that Dean William Gregory's actions were "unprofessional and vindictive in nature" and that a university has "no place for an individual, especially an administrator, who has little concern for the students and frustrates productive faculty members" (*Renken v. Gregory*, 541 F.3d 769, 772 [7th Cir.]). Citing *Garcetti*, the court held that "Renken made his complaints . . . pursuant to his duties as a University Professor" and therefore "his speech was not protected by the First Amendment" (*Id.* at 775). (The message: diss your dean at your peril.)

And in *Hong v. Grant* (2007), Juan Hong, a professor at the University of California at Irvine, contended that he was denied a merit raise "because of his critical statements regarding the hiring and promotion of other UCI professors as well as the use of lecturers to teach courses at the University." The court made short order of Hong's claim: "Because all of Mr. Hong's criticisms were made in the course of doing his job as a UCI professor, the speech is not protected from discipline by University administrators" (*Hong v. Grant*, 516 F. Supp. 2d 1158 [C.D. Cal.], 1160). The court refused to limit its holding and declared that "an employee's official duties are not narrowly defined, but instead encompass the full range of the employee's professional responsibilities." Anything a professor does "pursuant to official duties" is subject to the discipline of those he does it for. Indeed "even internal complaints about the employer's supervisory failures or workplace mismanagement are consistent with the type of activities the employee is professionally obligated to perform" (*Id.* at 1166). If, as a professor, you participate in reviews of your colleagues' performance or assess the qualifications of candidates as a member of a committee or express a concern about the number of lecturers the university employs (all activities Hong engaged in), you open yourself up to negative judgment because what you have undertaken to do "in a professional capacity" is to "further the employer's objectives," and the employer is the judge of whether you have done that satisfactorily (*Hong v. Grant*, 516 F. Supp. 2d. 1158, 1166). It is decisions like this one that led Joan DelFattore (2011) to declare that if the question is "whether administrative authority supersedes faculty free speech . . . the answer to that question has often been yes in the past, and is likely to remain so in the future."

The unwillingness of courts to constitutionalize intramural criticism follows from a general unwillingness to carve out exceptions for academics that are not granted to others. The right freely to criticize one's superiors is the very essence of academic exceptionalism because it is the right not to be bound by rules most workers are required to follow. Any defense of that claimed right must answer the question posed by Mark Yudof (1988): "The question is why academics, with respect to matters not directly related to teaching and scholarship, have a higher order of liberty in the workplace than others" (1355).

Matthew Finkin (1988) confronts the question directly by quoting a particularly forceful formulation of it: "Why would anyone have ever supposed that professors should have more liberty in the workplace than everyone else? Or, to state the question with its proper emphasis, why would anyone have ever supposed that everyone else should have weaker employee rights than college and university faculty" (1339). (We are back where we started on the first page of this book.) Finkin then objects to the form of the question, which he says "misapprehends the nature of the claim." The profession, he explains, "did not assert that *as employees* the professoriate had more rights than groundskeepers or food service workers" (emphasis in original). The assertion, rather, is that professors are not employees and therefore the relationship they have with their organizational superiors "should not be thought of in terms of an employment relationship *at all*." Consequently, "the special theory of academic freedom applied in the matter of intramural utterance neither depends upon nor is weakened by the absence (or presence) of a general theory of workplace rights" (1340; emphasis in original).

In short, forget about *Pickering, Connick, Urofsky*, and *Garcetti*; the situation of academics is entirely independent of those cases and of the tests they have put in place. This is an amazing sequence that amounts to saying, You want to know why academics are exempt from the rules that apply to other employees? Because they are not employees. And why are they not employees? Because they say so or, rather, because the AAUP's 1915 Declaration of Principles says so. As he elaborates this entirely circular argument, Finkin (1988) inevitably winds his way to a classic assertion of exceptionalism. He acknowledges that intramural criticism does not "contribute to the discovery of a disciplinary truth" (1342), and therefore that it "has nothing to do with the 'core' claim of freedom of disciplinary discourse" (1338); but, he says, universities, in addition to seeking truth, seek wisdom, and wisdom is a necessary ingredient of good administrative decisions. By engaging in intramural criticism when important matters are on the table, the professoriate refuses "to concede to the administration the possession of all wisdom on such matters" (1341).

Finkin's reasoning will appeal to any employee who believes (as each of us sometimes does) that he or she could make better decisions than a foreman or a manager or a dean. For most of us, however, the dream of stepping into the boss's shoes is a fantasy. Finkin and others of like mind believe that the realization of the fantasy is an academic right because academics are wiser than those who just happen to occupy high-level positions in the university's organizational hierarchy. With respect to their less-credentialed colleagues, they are exceptional.

Other Claims to Be Exceptional

I am poking fun at this position, but it has a long and honorable lineage beginning, as we have seen, with the AAUP's 1915 Declaration of Principles, where it is said firmly that professors "are the appointees, but not in any proper sense the employees" of university trustees and their deputies in the university administration. This bald declaration is an attempt, as Post (2006) points out, "to redefine the employment relationship between professors and universities" (62). The rule in 1915 (and still in some sectors of society today) was "employment-at-will," where the will referred to was the will of the employer, who could legally discharge his employees for cause or for no cause at all. It was occasions of discharge for no cause or for purely political cause that moved a group of distinguished academics to found the AAUP.

What the authors of the 1915 Declaration were trying to do, as Richard Hofstadter and Walter Metzger (1955) explain in their authoritative history of academic freedom, was appeal "to professors as professional men and not as employees" (478). The strategy was to bracket professors not with clerks and custodians, but with doctors, pastors, and lawyers who, while they work for hire, serve an enterprise larger than the interest of their local employers. Hence the famous analogy (cited earlier) of professors to judges: "University teachers should be understood to be, with respect to the conclusions reached and expressed by them, no more subject to the control of the trustees than are judges subject to the control of the president with respect to their decisions."

But notice how carefully formulated this is. Professors are not subject to control "with respect to the conclusions reached and expressed by them," but with respect to other matters—this is implied, not stated—professors are subject to the usual controls of a workplace; for it is "not the absolute freedom of utterance of the individual scholar, but the absolute freedom of thought, of inquiry, of discussion and of teaching, of the academic profession, that is asserted by this declaration of principles." Or in other words, render unto the administration what is the administration's, but when it comes to following the evidence where it leads, your responsibility is to the rigorous unfolding of critical inquiry. (Precisely the argument Kant makes in "What Is Enlightenment?")

This is the same formula offered in their own vocabularies by Yudof, Areen, Rabban, Horwitz, and Tepper and White, but Finkin (1988) isn't buying it:

> To concede the assumption of a master-servant relationship . . . , reserving the profession's claim of freedom of expression only to narrowly defined disciplinary discourse . . . would produce a profession in a sense "half slave" and "half free"—enjoying the freedom to teach that two and two are four conditioned upon maintaining a docile subservience to authority in intramural affairs. (1341)

The overheated rhetoric of this statement is continued and even ratcheted up in succeeding paragraphs, where we are told that unless your freedom to criticize extends to every aspect of university life, you are a mere hireling, a servant, and a sycophant (all words Finkin uses). Moreover you will lose your self-respect and the respect of your students: "A faculty that is perceived by its students as composed of frauds and fools is not likely to instill much love of learning or independence as a habit of mind" (1341). Absent the freedom of intramural criticism, the entire enterprise, Finkin implies, falls apart.

The same dire prediction turns up in discussions of the "press shield" invoked by journalists who claim "a First Amendment privilege that enables them to shield their sources and notes from disclosure in grand jury proceedings" (Weaver, Hancock, Lively, and Knechtle 2011, 587). The claim is both like and unlike the claim by academics to have special immunities that enable them to access pornographic materials while other cannot, and to have a special dispensation, indeed a duty, to criticize their institutional superiors in the harshest terms. First of all, the freedom the press invokes is named in the First Amendment while the Constitution is silent on academic freedom. Second, the claim by journalists to certain immunities is based on the nature of the job a free press is assigned in a democracy (to prevent the government from monopolizing and/or hiding the truth) and not on the virtue or wisdom of journalists. The job of the professoriate is much more parochial and less grandly ambitious. If I had to guess, I would say that given a choice between press freedom and academic freedom (of course no such choice is being forced) most Americans would choose press freedom.

Nonetheless, the Supreme Court has not been friendly to the request for a press shield law. (State courts have been more responsive.) The leading case is *Branzburg v. Hayes* (1972), where the Court declines "to grant newsmen a testimonial privilege that other citizens do not enjoy," despite the argument that "if forced to respond to subpoenas and identify their sources . . . , their informants will refuse or be reluctant to furnish newsworthy information in the future" (*Branzburg v. Hayes*, 408 U.S. 665, 690). The Court questions the empirical basis for this argument—"From the beginning of our country the press has operated without constitutional protection for press informants"—but its main point is categorical, not historical: "Newsmen are not exempt from the normal duty of appearing before a grand jury and answering questions relevant to a criminal investigation" (*Id.* at 685). The Court also rejects the fallback argument that the claimed privilege might be overridden by a showing of compelling interest: "If there is no First Amendment privilege to refuse to answer the relevant and material questions asked during a good-faith grand jury investigation, then it is a fortiori true that there is no privilege to refuse to appear before a grand jury until the Government demonstrates some 'compelling need' for a newsman's testimony" (*Id.* at 708).

It is also a fortiori true that if the courts are reluctant to grant special exemptions from generally applicable laws to journalists, they will be even more reluctant to grant them to academics. This is the explicit conclusion reached in a 2012 First Circuit case, *United States v. Moloney*: "If the reporter's interest were insufficient in Branzburg, the academic researchers' interests necessarily are insufficient" (*United States v. Moloney*, 685 F.3d 1). Two academic researchers were required by subpoena to turn over materials needed in connection with a murder investigation in the United Kingdom. (The British had requested and received cooperation from the US government). The researchers resisted, claiming "an academic research privilege to be evaluated under the same terms as claims of a reporter's privilege" (*Id.* at 16). The claim is summarily denied. "The choice to investigate criminal activity belongs to the government and is not subject to veto by academic researchers" (*Id.* at 19).

The logic the courts apply to what is known as the "ministerial exception" is exactly the reverse: what churches decide about matters pertaining to their organization and doctrine is not subject to veto by a generally applicable secular law. The ministerial exception gets a sympathetic hearing in the courts (at least at the present time) because it rests on a claim the advocates of press privilege and academic exceptionalism cannot make—the radical inability of courts as secular institutions to assess religious practices. You can study an academic subject and become knowledgeable about the ways and byways of the academy. You can go to journalism school or hang out with journalists and so acquire something like an insider's perspective. But learning about religion and immersing yourself in church history will not put you inside the religious experience, which is a matter not of empirical information or textbook knowledge, but of faith. (The dialogue between Faithful and Talkative in John Bunyan's *The Pilgrim's Progress* is an extended explication of the point.) Religion, like academic practice and the practice of journalism, is different; but religion is not only different, it is also special in a sense that academics and journalists vainly claim.

In *Hosanna-Tabor v. EEOC* (2012), now the leading case on the ministerial exception, the Supreme Court is explicit about its reason for not interfering "with an internal church decision that affects the faith and mission of the church" (*Hosanna-Tabor Evangelical Lutheran Church & Sch. v. EEOC*, 132 S. Ct. 694, 697). Cheryl Perich had returned from disability leave to find that her employer, the school of a Missouri Synod Lutheran Church, wished her to resign. She refused and filed a charge with the EEOC, alleging a violation of her rights under the Americans with Disabilities Act. The church responded that by looking to an outside agency for a resolution to an internal dispute, she had violated the church's conflict resolution policy. She replied that the so-called policy emerged only late in the proceedings and was therefore a pretext for an unlawful dismissal. The Court reasons that assessing whether the cited policy was in fact a core component of church doctrine as claimed would involve a judicial inquiry into the tenets of Lutheranism. That the Court declines to do because it is not for the government to pronounce on church doctrine. The First Amendment, it concludes, "gives special solicitude to the rights of religious organizations" (*Id.* at 706).

Special solicitude is what the academy keeps asking for but not receiving except in a few cases like *Grutter v. Bollinger* (2003), where the majority accepts the "principle of student body diversity" as a basis for taking race into account in the admissions process of a law school despite acknowledging that the "core purpose of the Fourteenth Amendment was to do away with all imposed discrimination based on race" (*Grutter v. Bollinger*, 539 U.S. 306, 341). Noting that universities "occupy a special niche in our constitutional tradition," the Court announces that the University of Michigan Law School's judgment that the achievement of diversity "is essential to its educational mission is one to which we defer" (*Id.* at 329). In dissent, Justice Clarence Thomas demurs: "There is no basis for a right of public universities to do what would otherwise violate the Equal Protection Clause," a position the Court seems to move toward in the 2013 case *Fisher v. University of Texas at Austin* (*Id.* at 362 [Thomas, J., dissenting]).

The deference the Court extends to universities in *Grutter* has led Byrne (2006) to conclude that the case "represents a high-water mark for the recognition and influence of constitutional academic freedom" (929). A more measured conclusion might be that in *Grutter* the Court continues a tradition of deference that is more practical than constitutional. That tradition has been given the name "academic abstention," defined by Byrne (1989) as "the traditional refusal of courts to extend common law rules of liability to colleges where doing so would interfere with the college administration's good faith performance of its core functions" (323). As an illustration of the courts' habit of abstaining from interference in academic matters, Byrne quotes a nineteenth-century case *Pratt v. Wheaton College* (1866): "A discretionary power has been given to [college authorities] to regulate the discipline of their colleges in such a manner as they deem proper, and so long as their rules violate neither divine nor human law, we have no more authority to interfere than we have to control the domestic discipline of a father in his family" (*People ex rel. Pratt v. Wheaton Coll.*, 40 Ill. 186, 187). Rooted in custom, this grant of discretionary power is far weaker than a statutory rule or constitutional command. It goes along with the idea that colleges have an authority over their students that parallels the authority parents have over their children, and with the picture of a college as a bucolic retreat from the pressures and conflicts of a competitive world.

Justice William Rehnquist invokes just that image of college life when in *Board of Curators v. Horowitz* (1978) he rules against the appeal of a dismissed student who had requested a hearing: "The educational process is not by nature adversary; instead it centers around a continuing relationship between faculty and students. We decline to further enlarge the judicial presence in the academic community and therefore risk deterioration of many beneficial aspects of the faculty-student relationship" (*Bd. of Curators of Univ. of Missouri v. Horow-itz*, 435 U.S. 78, 90). Courts, he concludes, "are particularly ill equipped to evaluate academic performances" (*Id.* at 92).

Notice again that this admission of incapacity is not a rule of law. It depends on interlocking (sociological) assumptions about the nature of college life and the extent to which the academy is a "world apart." Were the force of those assumptions to weaken, courts could rethink their position and withdraw their deference, and there is no statute or constitutional clause that would prevent them from doing so. In fact, this had already begun to happen in *Healy v. James* (1972). Although Justice Lewis Powell, writing for the majority, begins by saying "We approach our task with special caution recognizing the mutual interest of students, faculty members, and administrators in an environment free from disruptive interference with the educational process," he is soon announcing that "state colleges and universities are not enclaves immune from the sweep of the First Amendment" (*Healy v. James*, 408 U.S. 169, 180). Acknowledging that the courts have at times deferred to the authority of school officials, Powell declares "Yet, the precedents of this Court leave no room for the view that . . . First Amendment protections should apply with less force on college campuses than in the community at large . . . and we break no new constitutional ground in reaffirming this Nation's dedication to safeguarding academic freedom" (*Id.* at 180).

This is more than a little ironic (though not on Powell's part). The academic freedom being affirmed and safeguarded in *Healy* is the freedom of members of Students for a Democratic Society to associate in the face of a college administration's decision to deny them recognition; but the assertion of this freedom comes at the expense of the freedom of universities to order their internal affairs. Academic freedom is being invoked in a way that diminishes its scope. The freedom of the academy has hardly been reaffirmed when the courts takes it upon themselves to say who gets academic freedom and who doesn't.

As Amy Gajda (2009) reports, Powell's statements in *Healy* presage the future. Even as the courts continued to pay a rhetorical deference to the authority of school officials, they were arrogating that authority to themselves. Nowadays, says Gajda, "courts feel free to enter and reorder from the ground up, parceling out the rights and obligations of each disputant down to the last dollar and school vocation." Indeed, in recent years "courts have intervened to police the boundaries of permissible criticism in peer review, to weigh how professors should hand back exams, and to direct which of two candidates should be installed as student government president" (234). The decline of the judicial practice of academic abstention, in combination with the increasing tendency of courts (in the Pickering-Connick-Garcetti line of cases) to regard "delivery of educational services" as no different from "the sale of a lawnmower" (Gajda 2009, 208), has greatly undercut the claim of academic exceptionalism. Of the five schools of academic freedom I have identified, the school of academic exceptionalism is, at the present writing, the weakest and the least likely to garner support either inside or outside the university unless it is disguised as something else. The disguise it usually wears, as we shall see, is that of virtue.

VIRTUE BEFORE PROFESSIONALISM
The Road to Revolution

It is one of the paradoxes of academic exceptionalism that although it is validated by the machinery of professionalism, it ends up repudiating and attacking that same machinery. Academic exceptionalism is at once a consequence of professionalism—the status of being exceptional is thought to come along with the advanced degree—and an assault on it. Academics go through a process of training and accreditation that confers on them (or so they tell themselves) a special measure of erudition and wisdom, and then they turn around and declare themselves independent of the structures that made them erudite and wise. Indeed those structures, which include mechanisms of training and discipline, reward and punishment, are more than occasionally declared to be destructive of the capacities they have produced.

Denis Rancourt
Denis Rancourt, the University of Ottawa physicist who was dismissed in part because he turned a course in environmental physics into a course on political activism, is a case in point. In his correspondence with Marc Jolicoeur, chairman of the university's board of governors, Rancourt spends several paragraphs rehearsing his profes-

sional credentials and he boasts that his scholarly accomplishments far exceed those of his critics. He says that his "research successes" had been expected because he had started his university career "under the prestigious NSERC University Research Fellow program," and he reports that he has "obtained the largest NSERC Strategic Project Grant ever obtained in the Faculty of Science" (letter of January 5, 2009, in author's personal files). "I am recognized," he declares, "as an expert in my profession."

But his defense and justification of his classroom practice involves the repudiation and demonization of the profession whose honors he wears as a garland. He reports that in 2005, after many years "of observing classes that . . . served mainly to prepare students to be obedient and indoctrinated employees," he felt that he had to do "something more than give a 'better' physics course." That's when he came up with the idea of "academic squatting," the practice of taking an assigned course in a disciplinary subject and turning it into a course on political activism; not, he explains, a course about political activism, but a course that trains students to be activists (Rancourt 2007).

Giving a better physics course or a better Shakespeare course or a better contracts course is what academics of all stripes are trying to do; it is a widely shared professional goal. In detaching himself from that goal, Rancourt detaches himself from the profession, and as he does so he describes the profession he is leaving as a dehumanizing force that will take away your personhood in the course of pressing you into an "ideology of service." "Graduate or professional school," he declares on his Activist Teacher blog, "will rob you of you" and "you will be pushed to brainwash yourself into accepting . . . the established order at the expense of your moral values" (February 26, 2012). He identifies what he calls "the ideology of professionalism" with the erosion of "the natural impulse to learn" (August 11, 2007). You sell "your soul for a place in the sun," he writes. "Most students agree to give up their independence of thought and enquiry to serve the insane system of due dates and senseless assignments in exchange for the certificate" that stamps them as "persistently obedient" (August 11, 2007).

But there is something you can do, Rancourt tells students in a post on his blog: "Just stand up. Speak out. Confront. Others will join you." To be sure, such actions will bring you into conflict with the professional authorities and they will retaliate, but "if they are not coming after you then you are faking it" (February 26, 2012). That is, your authenticity will be measured by the degree to which you are rebuked and disciplined by the establishment. (Rancourt is here inviting students to join him in his favorite role of the heroic, beleaguered dissident.) While many professors talk a good solidarity-with-the-oppressed game, Rancourt charges that they stop far short of action. It is disgusting, he says in a post titled "Why we must despise university professors," "to observe university service intellectuals posturing themselves into a self-image of community service and solidarity with the oppressed-other while not raising a finger to dismantle the very machine at its core." Professors are "truly a disgusting breed" who "rise in the academic and administrative hierarchies for achieving emptiness and for celebrating emptiness." Consequently, "we must love humanity and freedom enough to despise them in liberating ourselves" (July 19, 2010).

Now remember that this is the same Rancourt who, in response to criticism, parades his professional credentials as a way of validating his status. How can he do that and at the same time trash the institution that provided those credentials? How can he disavow the "breed" of which he is himself a member? The answer is that like other antiprofessional professionals, Rancourt does not regard the abilities he now offers to democracy as having been produced by the educational system he excoriates. It may be true that he went through the training he warns students against, but unlike his too-tractable colleagues, he managed to go through the process without being contaminated and he came out on the other side with himself and his integrity intact. The expert knowledge he acquired along the way was just the gilding of a lily that was there already. That is why he can in good faith invoke the prestige of his professional degrees and publications when it is convenient (Why not take advantage of a corrupt system when you can?), and spend the rest of his time saying the worst things about the profession and professionalism he can think of.

That is also why he can cloak himself in the mantle of academic freedom at one moment and mount an all-out attack against it in the next. In the January 5, 2009, letter to Jolicoeur, Rancourt argues that his "pedagogical initiatives"—a nice phrase for the abandoning of pedagogy for political activism—were protected "by the accepted principle of academic freedom." A week later, in an interview at rabble.ca, he defines academic freedom as "the ideal under which professors and students are autonomous and design their own development and interactions" (Freeston 2009).

Just what, one might ask, are professors and students supposed to be autonomous *from*, and the answer is given when Rancourt contrasts his definition of academic freedom with another he rejects: "The institutions, however, define academic freedom to mean that the universities are not accountable to elected governments." The problem with this second definition, as far as Rancourt is concerned, is that under it freedom from accountability is given to universities and not to professors and students, who remain accountable to university rules and restrictions and far from free to "design their own development and interactions" (Freeston 2009). What Rancourt wants professors and students to be autonomous from is the university's monitoring of whatever they choose to do. In short, academic freedom means freedom from the academy. This, of course, is where the locating of academic freedom in the individual had always led. Rancourt just draws out the implications of that position in a manner that is unmistakable: if academic freedom is an important value, it's too important to be identified with or confined within the academy. So when academic freedom is put forward as a universal privilege, he embraces it; when academic freedom is put forward as a guild privilege, he trashes it.

This is made crystal clear when Rancourt responds to the question "Why should those outside of universities care about academic freedom?" They shouldn't, he says (in the rabble.ca interview), if the academic freedom in question is tied narrowly to the academy and its practices. To care about that "would imply the elitist notion that only university professors should have freedom of speech, freedom of inquiry and job security." Instead, he insists, all citizens should "fight for these principles in their own lives" because "all such fights create and strengthen political freedom for all" (Freeston 2009). In other words, academic freedom, insofar as it names something we should care about, must be a freedom enjoyed by everyone, which means that the adjective "academic," and with it the whole ethos of professionalism, is superfluous and should be discarded, as it is at the end of the sentence I have just quoted. Political freedom is what we are after, and if academic protocols do not contribute to its implementation, they must be cast aside in favor of the imperative of radical democracy, as Rancourt did when, to the distress of the university, he invited ten-year-olds to participate in his classes. After all, if you're training revolutionaries rather than scholars, it makes sense to get them early.

When I wrote briefly about Rancourt in the *New York Times*, some readers chided me for focusing on so extreme an example and presenting it as if his was a position held by more than a few crazies. But while Rancourt's pronouncements are theatrical and perhaps exaggerated for effect, the view underlying them is not that far, at least in its assumptions, from the views of Judith Butler and others who subordinate professional academic values to the value of critique. And, in fact, Rancourt's position has been ratified by an arbitrator commissioned in 2008 by the University of Ottawa and the Association of Professors of the University of Ottawa. Although he had critical things to say about the behavior of both parties, on the main point arbitrator Michel Picher sided with Rancourt in his report: "It is difficult for this arbitrator to conclude that it was inappropriate or beyond the bounds of academic freedom for Professor Rancourt to have framed the description of the course in the terms he chose" (http://www.archive.org/details/ArbitrationRuling-AcademicFreedom-ActivismCourse-UniversityOfOttawa).

This is as much to say that academic freedom has no bounds at all, except the bounds a professor chooses for himself. The Rancourt case is useful because it puts on display the steps by which taking a certain view of academic freedom leads to the expansion and consequent emptying out of the concept. If you begin by assuming that academic freedom attaches to the individual professor (and student) rather than to the institution, the exercise of your freedom might well involve flouting the institution's protocols in the name of a higher obligation; and once you reach that conclusion, you are more than halfway to deciding that what academics are free (and obligated) to do is critique and oppose arrangements that impede the advancement of social progress by protecting the status quo. It will then seem obvious to you that universities, tied as they are to the interests of the state and corporate capitalism, do just that kind of bad work. Therefore, in order to stand up for true freedom, you must burst the bounds of merely academic freedom and turn your energies against the structures that house you in the hope that, in time, they will be reformed and align themselves with the project of social justice. Academic freedom, in this logic, is appropriately exercised only when it transcends the academy and is no longer academic in any narrow sense.

The Boycott of Israeli Universities

Something very much like this sequence is enacted by those who have in recent years advocated a boycott of Israeli universities. They argue that because Israeli universities are funded by a rogue state and because the policies of that state have the effect of abrogating the academic freedom of Palestinian professors and students (by denying them materials, access, funding, and mobility), it is an expression, and not a violation, of academic freedom to refrain from engaging in intellectual commerce with Israeli universities or with Israeli scholars unless they actively repudiate the policies of their government. (I should note that whether the boycott should extend to individual scholars is a matter of dispute within the movement.)

"It is important to stress," declare the guidelines of the Palestinian Campaign for the Academic and Cultural Boycott of Israel (2009), "that all Israeli academic institutions, unless proven otherwise, are complicit in maintaining the Israeli occupation and denial of basic Palestinian rights." Pointing out that "Israeli universities are . . . heavily involved in tailored teaching for the military and security services," boycott supporters conclude that the "academic freedom of Israel has generated illegal, racist, and oppressive behavior [and] complicity in [the] government's expansionist and oppressive policies; and in response to the suffering imposed on the Occupied Territories and the violation of Palestinian academic freedom—deafening silence" (BRICUP 2007, 18–19). How, asks UCLA professor Sondra Hale, "can we discuss academic freedom in the absence of basic human rights?" (BRICUP 2007, 14). How will the invocation of academic freedom be received by Palestinian academics who live under conditions that make the phrase "meaningless":

> The destruction of infrastructure, civil society, and cultural and intellectual life cannot be separated from the question of academic freedom. The ability of teachers, researchers and students to deliver and access teaching cannot be separated from the question of academic freedom. The right to be free from arbitrary detentions and delays, and from the threat of an occupying force backed by the threat of violence cannot be separated from the question of academic freedom. (BRICUP 2007, 14)

The basic argument is that while academic freedom, conceived of narrowly as the freedom to engage in "scientific and scholarly discourse" without interference, is undoubtedly an "attractive" principle, it cannot be allowed to function as an alibi for the violation of principles of equal, and perhaps superior, importance. The point is made forcefully by Maximilian Forte (2009), associate professor of anthropology at Concordia University. Forte begins by wondering "how institutions that boast of enhancing and developing the individual's capacities for citizenship, for appreciation of diversity, and sensitivity to humanity, can so quickly turn a cold face to genocide." The path to the conclusion he wishes to reach is opened up the moment universities are made instrumental to extra-academic purposes. If individual growth, the formation of citizens, and the broad needs of humanity are identified as the university's core concerns, the freedom to teach, say, Byzantine Art and to publish scholarly monographs about it will seem pretty small potatoes; and a focus on such esoteric matters in a time of geopolitical urgency will be seen as a dereliction of duty.

Responding to a University of Ottawa professor's concern that a boycott would violate academic freedom, Forte deplores what he calls "a selfish and narrow way of thinking." Academic freedom, he declares, does not "trump everything else on earth." While in some respects academic freedom is "vital," it is not "so paramount that it rises above the interests of human beings subject to genocidal practices." Indeed, if given a choice, he "would rather live in a world with justice, and no concern with academic freedom, rather than the reverse." I cannot, he says, accept "the notion that out of concern for academic freedom, all other freedoms must be drowned." Political freedom must come before academic freedom, and any version of academic freedom that would draw a bright line separating academic work from political work must be rejected.

Forte correctly identifies the narrowness of an academic freedom understood as the freedom to engage in professional projects that stop at the water's edge of politics and address large-scale social concerns indirectly if at all. (What will a new account of *Paradise Lost* or of the doctrine of consideration in contract law do to alleviate human misery?) If the test universities must pass measures their contributions to world peace or universal justice, a university that sticks to its academic knitting will fail it, and Forte will be right to say "We should be serving humanity, be concerned for humanity, and [a university] ought to show more sensitivity and respect for humanity if it is to be taken seriously and to be protected as an institution worth preserving in very uncertain times."

In this argument, academic institutions deserve protection only if they detach themselves from merely professional academic imperatives and join the political struggle everyone should be engaged in. Like Rancourt, who, not surprisingly, supports the boycott, Forte is willing to invoke academic freedom as long as it is extended to everyone and not clung to as a guild privilege: "If academic freedom is what really mattered in this discussion, it would be made to matter for all, and not just held as the inviolable, paramount, and absolute right of a privileged few." This can't mean that everyone should be an academic, festooned with degrees and assigned an office in a university building. It must mean, rather, that everyone should enjoy the privileges and respect now accorded only to academics, everyone should be regarded as an equal partner in the struggle for social justice, everyone's contribution should be taken seriously, and everyone should be guaranteed the freedom to speak out without fear of retaliation. Needless to say, this utopian vision would spell the end of academic freedom as a doctrine responsive to the distinctive conditions—there wouldn't be any—of academic labor.

Still, it is not difficult to understand the appeal of this vision. The contention that in the end human freedom trumps academic freedom, if only because absent the security of human rights academic rights can neither flourish nor be protected, seems intuitively right. It is a matter of what comes first, isn't it? As Omar Barghouti (2011) explains, the "privileging of academic freedom as a super-value above all other freedoms is in principle antithetical to the very foundation of human rights" (105). If an oppressive regime makes daily life miserable for an entire population, including its students and teachers, and if you determine that fellow academics flourishing under that regime are either passive or complicit, isn't it your duty—both as a professor and as a human being—to apply what leverage you have in an effort to provoke your delinquent colleagues to rouse themselves and do the right thing? If you fail to do so, do you not join them in their complicity? Isn't it simply wrong to hunker down in the academic trenches, writing your essays and teaching your sanitized classes, while millions are denied the freedom you take for granted?

On the other side—the side I favor—there is only one thing to say and it amounts largely to a reaffirmation of the independence and priority of professional academic values. I don't mean that professional values take precedence over more general human values, but that more general human values should not be the ones dictating your behavior when you are acting as a professional. In 2002, Mona Baker, a professor of translation studies at the University of Manchester in England, removed two Israelis from the editorial boards of the journals *Translator* and *Translation Studies Abstracts*. She told a reporter that she wasn't boycotting Israelis, just "Israeli Institutions," and in an e-mail to Gideon Toury, one of those she had "unappointed," she declared that she continued to regard him as a friend, and that her decision was "political, not personal." (All too true.) Toury replied, "I would appreciate it if the announcement made it clear that 'he' (that is, I), was appointed as a scholar and unappointed as an Israeli" (the correspondence is posted on Baker's website: www.monabaker .com). In other words, when you invited me it was by virtue of my scholarly credentials, with no concern for my nationality or religious affiliations, and now you disinvite me for political reasons, reasons that are not relevant to the doing of academic business.

Baker and Toury are not really in disagreement: each is aware that the boundaries separating academic judgments and political judgments—between academic reasons for appointing a board member and political reasons for appointing a board member—have been breached. It is just that while Toury continues to insist on the independent integrity of the academic community—a community that knows no geography but the metageography of professional recognition and cooperation—Baker would claim that the community's integrity cannot possibly be independent of the material conditions without which contemplative leisure is impossible. In her view, one must act politically so that those conditions can be restored.

Judith Butler (2006b) makes the same point: "academic freedom only gains its meaning within a broader conception of freedom on the condition that other basic political entitlements are first secured" (10). Butler's statement allows us to see clearly why the word "freedom" in the phrase "academic freedom" is the source of so much confusion. Freedom is obviously a political concept, and it is easy to make the mistake of thinking that something called academic freedom is a political value in competition with other political values to which it must, on occasion, yield. But the fact that academic freedom cannot flourish in a political space that denies the conditions necessary for its exercise does not mean that academic freedom is a political value. It is an abstract value—the value of the unfettered search for truth—and it is defined independently of the political circumstances that might attend or frustrate its implementation. Those circumstances, whether encouraging or discouraging of the value, are not essential to it as distinct from being essential to its realization. Butler says that "it makes no sense to value the doctrine in the abstract if we cannot call for its implementation" (11). But it makes the same sense as valuing universal health care apart from the question of whether the political/economic situation of a particular nation is such that the care can actually be delivered. If it were determined that the actions of nation X had the effect of undermining the health care of nation Y's citizens, would we then think it right to refuse to sell medical supplies to nation X in the hope that the damage to *its* citizens would provoke a reconsideration of policy? The value—whether it be academic freedom or universal health care—is one thing, the context of its instantiation another; and when one context has been rendered inhospitable to the value (perhaps by an occupation), the conclusion cannot be to abandon it by surrendering it to politics. Boycotters who say "because the Israelis deny academic freedom to the Palestinians, we're going to deny it to them" are also denying it to themselves. They reason that given the present circumstances we cannot continue to respect the distinctiveness of academic work — a distinctiveness defined by its difference from political work — and we are morally obligated to use the leverage provided by our academic positions to perform political acts. They congratulate themselves for doing a good deed while happily paying the price for their virtue of abandoning the academic integrity they continue to claim.

No doubt Butler would resist my critical account of the boycotters' logic. "We could say," she writes dismissively, "that these are material devastations and ought to be addressed by other means, but that, strictly speaking, these are not matters of academic freedom" (2006b, 11). "Strictly speaking" in Butler's vocabulary means speaking within a pinched, narrow position in which the discourse of academic freedom proceeds merrily and airily along while entire populations are unable to exercise the freedom being celebrated (a version of Nero fiddling while Rome burns). That is the position held by those (like me) for whom academic freedom is a professional concept that is not enlarged but hollowed out when it becomes the freedom (and the duty) to act in extraprofessional ways.

Butler is quite precise in her characterization of both what is asked and perhaps lost by such strict speaking: "If to enter the debate on academic freedom is precisely to bracket out . . . the material devastations characteristic of the Occupation, . . . then what form of political constriction is performed through constricting the discourse of academic freedom to a narrow liberal conception?" (2006b, 16). The assertion of her dependent clause ("If to enter") is correct: the narrow liberal conception of academic freedom does bracket out many important geopolitical questions. But the bracketing out is not a self-consciously performed act of turning one's back on "terrible circumstances." That is, as an academic you don't say to yourself, I am now going to put aside the devastations of the Occupation (or of Sudan or of Syria or of a hundred other places) and just focus on medieval metrics or the Hundred Years War. Once you step into the world where topics like these are the basis of a lifetime of scholarly work, the putting-aside (at least for the period of professional labor) has already occurred, not as an act of the will—you don't pledge to close your eyes to the suffering of peoples—but as the consequence of your having committed yourself (again for certain specified times, not all the time) to a necessarily limited project, the project of engaging in the practices that typically take place in universities.

Of course, this is a choice—no one forced you to become an academic—and one could argue that, on a very general level, the choice is a political one. You could decide, as many have, that life is too short to spend a significant amount of it worrying over something perhaps only five hundred other people in the world care about. You could decide to leave the academy and devote all your energies to, say, the redressing of injustice and the alleviation of misery. But if instead you decide to stay, you should stay wholeheartedly and not sail under false colors by appropriating the machinery and prestige of the academy for political purposes, as Rancourt frankly urges and Butler urges in effect.

But isn't deciding to stay a political act too? No, deciding to stay is deciding to do one job rather than the many others you could do if you left. The answer to Butler's question—"What form of political constriction is performed through restricting the discourse of academic freedom to a narrow liberal conception?"—is "No form at all." Restricting the discourse of academic freedom to a "narrow conception" is simply to recognize that academic work, like every other kind of work, *is* narrowly conceived. No kind of work does everything and a task whose limits are expanded far beyond what appropriately belongs to it (and I know that "appropriateness" is precisely what is in dispute) is no longer what it is. Choosing to perform a limited task and determining to respect its limits is not a political statement; it is a professional statement. The politics, as I have already said, comes in earlier, when you decide to perform this task rather than another. Fidelity to your decision to be a professional, not a constricting of your politics, is what is being practiced.

Nor will it do to say (as Butler sometimes seems to) that demarcating a space where analysis and description but not politics (in the partisan sense) are done is itself a political act for which one must take responsibility. This argument, which continues to be popular in certain quarters, gets its apparent force by enlarging the category of politics until it includes everything: urging specific policies is political and ruling out the urging of specific policies is political. But expanding the meaning of politics in this fashion is just like expanding the meaning of academic freedom until it encompasses anything an academic might think right to do; the concept loses its usefulness as a way of making distinctions (which is of course the strategy of those who equate academic freedom with critique and revolution).When Butler calls for a "more robust conception of academic freedom" (16), one that does not rule out the debating of political matters with a view to deciding them, she is calling for the end of the academy as a place where a distinctive activity is performed and advocating instead for a place indistinguishable at bottom from the ballot-box, the parliamentary debate, and the street rally.

Now an argument that there should not be an academy and that society's resources and the energies of citizens would be better expended elsewhere is an argument I am always ready to entertain. I have never been a hard-core defender of the educational experience or of disinterested inquiry as a value that must be protected at all costs. All I would say is that if we are going to have an academy we should really have it in all its glorious narrowness and not transform it into an appendage of politics, even when—no, especially when—the politics is one we affirm and believe in with all our hearts.

A Summing Up

As a way of bringing this part of our discussion to a close, let us revisit the taxonomy of the schools of academic freedom and ask what each of them would say about the boycott of Israeli universities and scholars. (Much of the answer has been anticipated.)

(1) The "It's just a job" school would see the boycott as a perfect example of what happens when the narrowly professional conception of academic work is enlarged so that its exercise can be directly linked to "real world" problems and their possible solutions. Even the apparently innocuous tying of academic freedom to democracy leads to an alteration in the direction of justification; for rather than asking how a proposed project contributes to the furthering of knowledge, one asks how the project furthers the goals of democracy. Sooner or later, that question will be seen as legitimizing any action taken by academics in the name of social justice, and boycotting Israeli universities will be regarded as the fulfillment of academic freedom rather than as its violation (precisely the argument of the boycotters).

(2) The boycott presents a difficult problem for the "For the common good" school, which is in many ways a "swing" school. As I observed earlier, the shift from the professional good to the common good opens the door to the transformation of academic freedom into an agenda of political activism, and that is a door members of the "For the common good" school are reluctant to walk through. So they are pulled in two directions, affirming professional norms while leaning toward the norms and imperatives of a progressive politics. Thus the split message of the 2006 American Association of University Professors (AAUP) statement on academic boycotts.

The statement begins by reaffirming the AAUP's 2005 resolution: "We reject proposals that curtail the freedom of teachers and researchers to engage in work with academic colleagues, and we reaffirm the paramount importance of the freest possible international movement of scholars and ideas" (AAUP 2006). But then the statement goes on to acknowledge candidly that the AAUP's practices have not always been faithful to its own severe standard. In 1970 the organization engaged in a debate about whether a university should "take a position on disputed public issues" like the Vietnam War. One side said no, reasoning that a university should not "become an instrument of indoctrination." The other side argued that there should be an exemption for "extraordinary situations." The question of dealing with German universities under the Nazis was raised: "Can one plausibly maintain that academic freedom is inviolate when the civil freedoms of the larger society have been abrogated?" (AAUP 2006) (This, you will recall, is a key argument in the repertoire of anti-Israeli boycotters.)

Fifteen years after the AAUP debate over Vietnam the same issues surfaced in the context of the movement to divest from companies doing business with South Africa. In a 1985 resolution, the AAUP called on colleges and universities to "oppose apartheid" by declining "to hold securities in banks which provide loans to the government of South Africa." This, it was said, "did not constitute an academic boycott" because it kept open "lines of communication among scholars in accordance with principles of academic freedom." By thus splitting hairs, the organization was able to claim that it "carefully distinguished between economic and academic boycotts largely on matters of principle" (AAUP 2006), although one could argue that the so-called principle failed the test of "indirect effect": an economic boycott is likely to have an adverse impact on teachers and researchers.

It is in the context of this ambiguous history that the AAUP confronted the calls for a boycott of Israeli universities. This time it appeared to come down squarely against boycotts: "In view of the Association's long-standing commitment to the free exchange of ideas, we oppose academic boycotts." But then the report concluded with a curious sentence the two halves of which are much closer together than its syntax suggests: "We understand that threats to or infringement of academic freedom may occasionally seem so dire as to require compromising basic precepts of academic freedom, but we resist the argument that extraordinary circumstances should be the basis for limiting our fundamental commitment to the free exchange of ideas and their free expression" (AAUP 2006). Huh? The argument "we" resist after the "but" is the argument whose force "we" acknowledge in the part of the sentence before the "but." We concede X, but we resist X.

The fence sitting this sentence performs is characteristic of the 2006 statement as a whole, especially its list of alternative "sanctions and protests," short of boycott, that might be considered by the university community as a response to Israeli aggression—"resolutions by higher education organizations condemning violations of academic freedom whether they occur directly by state or administrative suppression of opposing points of view or indirectly by creating material conditions such as blockades, checkpoints, and insufficient funding of Palestinian universities, that make the realization of academic freedom impossible" (AAUP 2006). The adverb "indirectly" lets in everything the firm stand against boycotts supposedly bars. If universities can legitimately issue condemnations and sponsor protests whenever the actions of a state indirectly affect academic freedom adversely, the line separating academic and political actions has been irremediably blurred.

The same blurring of the line occurs in a widely read 2007 essay by Martha Nussbaum, an AAUP-style liberal. Though the article is titled "Against Academic Boycotts," she writes that she too believes that there are "a number of options open to those who want to express strong condemnation." She lists several of them, beginning with "censure": "a professional association might censure an academic institution that violates the rights of scholars." (That of course is the job of AAUP Committee A). That seems straightforward enough, as does the option of "organized public condemnation." Nussbaum illustrates this tactic by declaring that "if Martin Heidegger had been invited to the University of Chicago, I would have been one of the ones conducting a public protest of his appearance and trying to inform other people about his record of collaboration with the Nazi regime" (32). I probably would not have been one of those protesting Heidegger's appearance, but that is neither here nor there because the university would have been allowing, not sponsoring, our respective responses to the prospect of his visit. That is the proper balance for a university to strike: it should provide a venue for the expression of different points of view, but favor none of them. As long as the "organized public condemnation" is not being organized by the institution, the participation of individual professors (acting in the public square, not in the classroom) leaves the distinction between academic and political work intact.

But the wall separating academic from political activity is breached when Nussbaum announces as another "option" (short of boycotting) open to a university—the "failure to reward." The institution, she says, "might decide that [an] individual does not deserve special honors," such as an honorary degree. Her example is Margaret Thatcher, who, she says, was understandably denied an honorary degree from Oxford because by "conferring an honorary degree, a university makes a strong statement about its own values" (34). No, it doesn't. By conferring an honorary degree, a university recognizes the significance—in the sense of magnitude—of the recipient's labors; it does not endorse them. A university that awarded a degree to either Antonin Scalia or Ruth Bader Ginsburg would not be indicating approval of the honoree's decisions; it would be recognizing that in their professional capacities these justices have played a significant role in shaping the nation's legal culture.

Failure to make this distinction informed the opposition at Southern Methodist University to housing the George W. Bush presidential library. The protestors confused the question "Is the tenure of a two-term U.S. president a worthy subject of academic study?" (a rhetorical question with only one possible answer) with the question "Do we politically and morally approve of the president's policies?", a question a university should neither ask nor answer. When Nussbaum declares that Thatcher's "assault on basic scientific research" in addition to her "ruin of the national medical system" were "values that the Oxford faculty believed that it could not endorse," she falls into the same confusion. Oxford faculty members would not have been endorsing Thatcher's policies by acquiescing in the awarding of a degree to her; they would have been testifying to her immense and undoubted stature as a national and world figure. At this point one might object that the same could be said about Al Capone or Adolf Hitler; but Capone and Hitler were criminals and (in different ways and on different scales) mass-murderers. One can still hold on to the category of "significant figure" as a basis for selection while excluding from it the performance of significant criminality. (To be sure the distinction isn't always perspicuous; while some regard Henry Kissinger as an exemplary statesman, others think of him as a war criminal.)

Nussbaum (2007) slides further down the slippery slope when she declares that under the rubric of "failure to reward" "one might, in some cases of competition for merit grants, refuse to reward Israel, without endorsing a boycott." Surely that is a distinction without a difference: excluding Israeli academic institutions from a competition for funds is just a boycott by another name. Nussbaum's alternative options, like those listed in the AAUP's 2006 statement, illustrate how easy it is for members of the "For the common good" school to cross the line that separates academic work from political advocacy. If you take your eyes off the academic ball even for a minute and look upward to the vistas of the common good, it will be only a matter of time before the common good swallows the academic good. Once you allow your passion for social justice to be even a small ingredient in your academic decisions, once you extend invitations or disburse funds on the basis of political judgments, no matter how high-minded, the argument against boycotts—the argument Nussbaum wants to make—is without a ground.

(3) There is no straight line from the "Academic exceptionalism" school ("academic freedom is for uncommon beings") to any position on the boycott of Israeli institutions and scholars. Exceptionalism, as we have seen, is typically asserted in the context of employment disputes; the claim is that academics

should be exempt from regulations and limitations to which other workers are bound. One could affirm that claim and have any view, or no view, of the boycott.

(4) The relationship between the "critique" school of academic freedom and approval of the boycott is much closer, and is indeed inherent in the notion of critique itself. At least as it is urged by members of this school, critique is inseparable from the quest for social justice. Henry Giroux (2010) calls this quest, as it is conducted in the university, "critical pedagogy": "Critical pedagogy is about providing the conditions for students to be agents in a world that needs to be interrogated as part of a broader project of connecting the search for knowledge, truth, and justice to the ongoing tasks of democratizing both the university and the larger society" (31). It is important for this school that the "interrogation" not be merely academic, as it is, for example, in some safely theorized versions of postmodernism. The relevant distinction is made by Sophia A. McClennen (2010): "The key nuance between postmodern political critique and postmodern apolitical critique is that in the former questions are posed in the service of struggle and vision, and in the latter, the questions are an end in themselves" (209). Posing questions as ends in themselves leaves everything in the world just as it was before the questioning began; posing questions in order to arrive at answers that will dictate corrective action is a contribution to "struggle," not a mere meditation on it.

The point of critique, McClennen is saying, should be not to contemplate the shape of political conditions, but to alter them. It follows that rather than being opposed to academic freedom, the boycott of Israeli universities is demanded by academic freedom, at least insofar as academic freedom is identified with the exercise of politically effective—not merely academic—critique. To invoke academic freedom as a prophylactic device for stopping boycotters in their path is to turn a potentially powerful doctrine into a rationale and excuse for doing nothing while the freedom of your brothers and sisters is being laid waste. "There can be . . . no demand that Israeli academics not be denied academic freedom when such freedom is routinely, deliberately, and as a matter of state policy, denied to their Palestinian colleagues" (Farred 2008–2009, 354). Once again academic freedom is "saved" by refusing to limit its scope and obligations to the academy. In a statement I quoted at the beginning of this book, Grant Farred identifies the imperative that follows from the installation of active, not merely intellectual, critique at the center of academic freedom: "Academic freedom has to be conceived as a form of political solidarity" (355).

(5) Once that conception is in place, the school of "Academic freedom as revolution" has been fully realized. In fact, it would be no exaggeration to say that the boycott of Israeli institutions *is* the realization of this school, for it involves a deliberate and unapologetic turning of the energies of the academy *against* the academic project, at least insofar as that project confines itself to asking and answering narrowly professional questions. The boycott, as Farred's pronouncement makes clear, represents the overwhelming of traditional academic concerns by blatantly political concerns. The boycott is academic squatting writ large: not just a single course, but the entire project, is hijacked for political ends.

I know that by reaching that conclusion I invite the argument that is always made (I have made it myself) against any claim that a realm is, or could be, purged of politics—the argument that no area of experience, not even a supposedly politics-free zone, escapes politics. R. Radhakrishnan (2008–2009) puts it this way:

Is the world out there and is academia an interior space? Isn't the world somehow always already in, and isn't academia always in a relationship of heteronomous exteriority to the world of which it is a representation/ mediation? Aren't outsides and insides always reciprocally relational and mutually constitutive such that there can be no absolute and non-negotiable forms of exteriority and interiority? (505)

I cheerfully stipulate to the assertions implicit in Radhakrishnan's questions. If the academy is an interior space it is so only by permission of the outside it defines itself against; and, moreover, that outside—the world with all its political/ economic/cultural forces and biases—rather than being excluded from the interior space from which it only rhetorically withdraws, configures it and everywhere marks it. The outside owns the inside and, therefore, the claim of the academy to be an inside—to be sharply distinguishable from what it pushes away, to be an independent, pure thing—cannot be maintained. There is no "intrinsic" form of the academy, only the form that emerges when some historically limited, contestable definitions and demarcations are put in place by an act of the will. There is, I must acknowledge, no reason in nature for the category of academic work not to include the direct taking up of charged political questions with a view to pronouncing on them and thus prompting students to action. The academy I defend in these pages—narrowly professional and resistant to calls for "relevance"—cannot be defended down to the ground; it rests on foundations no firmer than its self-assertion and the putting into place of the practices it calls for.

Butler (2009), then, is right when, in a critique of Kant, she insists that philosophy's "claim to transcendental status"—its claim to rise above politics—can be maintained only "by virtue of its implication in politics." She asks, "Is it a transcendental ground that conditions philosophy's difference . . . , or is it precisely the way that line of demarcation is drawn that produces the transcendental effect upon which the disciplinary self-definition of philosophy depends" (782). (Do line drawings trace out and make visible preexisting distinctions or are the distinctions brought into being by the arbitrary drawing of lines?) Butler's question could be rephrased. "Is it a transcendental ground that conditions the academy's difference, or is it precisely the way that line of demarcation is drawn that produces the difference upon which the academy's self-definition depends?" Both Butler and I would affirm the second alternative. It is "the particular political power of delimitation"—

the bald declaration that there politics is and here it is not—and nothing more foundational that produces the differences which then offer themselves as essential and justified by the nature of things.

We disagree, however, in our assessment of whether this production of an artificial difference is a good or bad thing. For Butler (2009) it has the unfortunate effect of creating an area "in which critique ought not to go." The academy gains its internal coherence at the price of being unable either to interrogate its boundaries or to move beyond them to a direct engagement with the world: "If, according to the Kantian scheme, philosophy has held itself exempt from state commands and policies, then philosophy has been instrumental in limiting the scope of critique" (782). To which I would reply, "Yes, and it does that in order to be what it is." What Butler complains about—the limitation of critique in the academy to the realm of thought—I see as the necessary founding gesture of the academic space. If, in the words of Kant (1798), it is essential that there be a learned community that "having no commands to give is free to evaluate everything," the only way to establish that community is, first, to declare it into existence, and, then, to enforce the distinctions that sustain its entirely arbitrary vision (27).

It is because the vision is arbitrary—not motivated by an authority higher or more foundational than itself—that its maintenance is entirely an internal responsibility. If members of the academy wish to continue doing what they have been trained to do—turn the lens of disinterested inquiry on the objects of its attention—it is up to them to monitor the conditions that ensure the health of their practice. That practice is not underwritten by any theory of truth (even though truth is the standard and goal that impel it forward) and it will not survive an interrogation that demands an independent corroboration of its cogency. It is underwritten only by its own protocols and if they are flouted or actively rejected, the activity they make possible will disappear. The professional definition of academic freedom is not merely a rival account of the academy. It *is* the academy. A capacious definition of academic freedom, urged in the name of social justice and human solidarity, undermines both academic freedom and the very idea of academic life.

I am aware that the argument I am making here is a hybrid, perhaps even a monster. I combine an antifoundationalist epistemology with an insistence on maintaining a foundational structure that is, by my own admission, artificial, historically emergent and, therefore, challengeable; and I do so in the conviction that without such a foundation—supported by nothing but itself—a certain mode of experience will be lost. The next question is, "So what if it were lost"? Without invoking an external justification of the kind I've been resisting, that is a question I cannot answer.

A final note. Although the campaign to boycott Israeli universities has gained some traction in England and other European countries, until recently it had made little headway in the United States. That changed somewhat in 2013 when the Association for Asian American Studies and the American Studies Association passed resolutions in favor of the boycott. And then in the first ten days of 2014, the Delegate Assembly of the much larger Modern Language Association put forward a resolution (not yet voted on by the entire membership at this writing) condemning Israel for "denials of entry to the West Bank by U.S. academics who have been invited to teach, confer, or do research at Palestinian universities." This is, to be sure, a far cry from endorsing a boycott, but some believe that an endorsement will be the next step. Others are doubtful. We shall see.

What is not in doubt is the political—not academic—nature of the boycotters' reasoning. In a question-and-answer statement posted online, the ASA rehearses its political—again, not academic—bona fides: "The ASA has long played an important role in critiquing racial, sexual, and gender inequality. . . . It has condemned anti-immigration discrimination in Arizona. . . . It has spoken out in support of the Occupy movement and of the human rights and dignity of the economically

disenfranchised" (www.theasa.net/what_does_the_academic
_boycott_mean_for_the_asa/). Given that record of politically inspired actions, it is no surprise that the organization
would line up behind the boycott, described in its statement
as a contribution "to the larger movement for social justice."
The question of why a supposedly academic entity is expend-
ing its energy and influence on this or any other "movement"
is not asked, but the answer is obvious. The ASA, by its own
admission, has long since ceased to be an academic entity. This
is made absolutely clear by ASA member Steven Salaita, who
is quoted as saying, "American studies as a discipline is really
preoccupied with issues of race and racism and colonization
and so I feel like the resolution is very much in keeping with
the sorts of things that a larger number of American studies
scholars focus on in their research" (Redden 2013). There is a
difference—the very difference proclaimed by Max Weber in
"Science as a Vocation"—between focusing in a scholarly way
on a topic that raises important political issues and taking a
position on those issues in a manner that demands and leads
to overt political actions, like the action of joining a boycott.
This is the difference Salaita happily elides and it is my thesis
in this book that if you elide that difference, academic work
and life will not have been enhanced or made more significant;
they will have disappeared.

I cannot conclude without taking up another question many readers will have been asking. Doesn't a narrowly professional guild account of the academy and academic freedom trivialize a noble human enterprise? Isn't there more to what we academics do than merely protecting our independence and maintaining the integrity—by which I mean ivory-tower purity—of the enterprise? Isn't Edward Said (1994) right when he insists that a true intellectual is not a professional, but "an amateur, someone who considers that to be a thinking and concerned member of a society one is entitled to raise moral issues at the heart of even the most technical and professionalized activity as it involves one's country, its power, its mode of interacting with its citizens as well as with other societies" (82)? Doesn't what we do have a social value, and shouldn't we be explaining ourselves in terms of that value?

As we have seen, one answer to these questions has been given by Robert Post and others who assert a strong relationship between academic freedom and the flourishing of democracy. J. Peter Byrne (2009) argues in this vein when he says that "Fish offers an impoverished defense of higher education by denying its social value" and failing to take note of the fact that it "is imbedded in a democratic society upon which it depends for financial, moral, and political support" (157). Having given that support, society, Byrne explains, naturally expects something in return: "federal programs and the historic generosity of state legislatures have always been justified by the contributions to the practical value of new . . . knowledge." The health and viability of the academy depends on the public's believing "that giving faculty their professional freedom will result in valuable knowledge and a better prepared citizenry." After all, Byrne observes, "if academic practices have no relation to larger concerns of life, why should a trustee, taxpayer, or parent provide resources to carry them on?" (157).

Why, indeed! As an account of the likely basis for society's support of the academy, what Byrne says rings true, but it has nothing to do, necessarily, with what is distinctive about the academy. It is a truth about the justifying of higher education—always an effort performed on a public stage—not a truth about the constitutive value of higher education. Higher education is not valuable because of the benefits some nonacademics might see in it; that's like valuing the theater or art because they bring people into the inner city. Higher education is valuable (if it is) because of the particular pleasures it offers to those who are drawn to it—chiefly the pleasures of solving puzzles and figuring out what makes something what it is—pleasures that would be made unavailable or rendered secondary if higher education were regarded as the extension of another enterprise. One should not mistake an understanding of why something is supported for an understanding of what that something is.

Nor should one confuse the reasons that lead society to pay for an activity with the reasons that impel its practitioners to engage in it. One set of reasons follows from the dynamics of persuasion: What appeals are likely to garner support? The other set of reasons follows from one's commitment to a way of life: What can I do that will fulfill me and realize my capacities to the fullest? Of course, it may be the case that the reasons others have for valuing your work sometimes dovetail with the reasons that motivate your doing of it, but that would just be a happy accident. Academics would still be doing what they do even if a democracy-related defense of higher education had never been mounted. The public may, as Byrne says, "desire . . .

socially valuable outcomes," but what academics desire are academically valuable outcomes (157). The rest is gravy.

Byrne offers a second societal justification for supporting the academy. As the exercise of rationality, academic work teaches "people to engage arguments independently," and its methods are "essential learning for the leaders in the kind of society we wish to be" (158). I do not deny that society's leaders may have acquired some useful political skills in the course of their university education, but the imparting of those skills was not what their instructors had in mind. Byrne speculates that "students studying Milton with Professor Fish will learn the sophisticated questions and methods of contemporary literary criticism, but they also will learn more generally how to make and critique arguments about their cultural tradition" (158). Some will, some won't. All I want my students to learn are the ways and byways of literary study; what they may learn "more generally" is not something that can be designed, even though one may wish for it. If it happens, it is an extra added benefit, an unsought-for plus, not the heart and soul of the enterprise. The university may be, as Byrne says, "a holy place for a liberal society," but for faculty and students it's a place where you teach and learn things (158). End of story.

But there is another objection to that story as I tell it: not the objection that it leaves higher education without a firm (as opposed to contingent) relation to a social value, but the deeper objection that it reduces academic work to a set of routines performed in obedience to norms backed up by nothing more than the fact that they happen to be in place. Where's the overarching norm that both legitimates the day-to-day norms and provides a basis for their possible correction? (We are back to Butler's worry.) I believe that I have answered that question, but the answer may have been obscured by my insistence throughout on a deflationary, severely professional account of the academy and academic freedom. Let's go back to the beginning and revisit my basic argument.

The academy is the place where knowledge is advanced, where the truth about matters physical, conceptual, and social is sought. That's the job, and that's also the aspirational norm: the advancement of knowledge and the search for truth. The values of advancing knowledge and discovering truth are not extrinsic to academic activity; they constitute it. They are the "internal goods" the "shared pursuit" of which holds the community together as its members strive for the "satisfaction of authoring first-rate literary criticism or an outstanding ethnography or an elegant mathematical paper" (Post 2009, 768). These goods and values are also self-justifying in the sense that no higher, supervening, authority undergirds them; they themselves undergird and direct the job and serve as a regulative ideal in relation to which current ways of doing things can be assessed and perhaps reformed. (The "It's just a job" school is not positivism; it does not reify what is on the books.)

It follows from this specification of the academy's internal goods that the job can be properly done only if it is undistorted by the interests of outside constituencies—constituencies that have something other than the search for truth in mind. There are thus limits both on the influences academics can properly respond to and the concerns they can take into account when doing their work. So, for example, public opinion cannot be an ingredient in academic judgment (although it can be a subject of academic study) because public opinion is a measure of what a majority of persons happens to believe rather than a measure of truth. While there are no limits to the subjects academics can investigate—the truth of anything can be inquired into—there are limits to the controlling motives within which investigation is to be conducted. It must be conducted (to return to the American Association of University Professors' 1915 Declaration of Principles) "in a scholar's spirit," that is, with a view to determining what is in fact the case and not with a view to affirming a favored or convenient conclusion. If that is the spirit that animates your academic work, you should be left free to do it, although, with respect to other parts of the job (conforming to departmental protocols, showing up in class, teaching to the syllabus), you are properly constrained.

That's it in a nutshell, but there is a next step that may seem unwarranted and vulnerable to Butler-like objections. That is the step that goes from the insistence that one should be doing truth seeking and not politics in the classroom—one should not appropriate the pedagogical space for partisan purposes as William Robinson did—to the insistence that political matters shouldn't be debated in the classroom *as such*. It is perfectly OK to debate the logic and cogency of the various positions on a political matter as long as the debate is not meant to lead to a resolution: let's do this rather than that. The problem is that there is surely a truth about political matters just as there is a truth about literary, economic, sociological, and mathematical matters. If unconstrained inquiry into the truth is the overarching academic norm, why is seeking the truth about a political matter currently in dispute out of bounds? Why should there be constraints on the kind of truth that is being sought in a classroom? As an instructor, why can't you ask, "Is it true that we should withdraw from Afghanistan tomorrow?" or "Should we move against Iran before it has an atomic capability?", while you can ask (at least by my lights), "Is Satan the hero of *Paradise Lost*?" or "Was the Civil War fought for economic rather than moral reasons?"

One answer to these questions is given by Aristotle, when, at the conclusion of the *Nicomachean Ethics*, he distinguishes between the active and the contemplative life. Of the latter he says, "This activity alone would seem to be loved for its own sake; for nothing arises from it apart from the contemplating, while from practical activities we gain more or less apart from the action." Practical activities have their reward from their consequences; contemplative activities are their own reward and are therefore superior. "The activity of reason, which is contemplative, seems both to be superior in serious worth and to aim at no end beyond itself, and to have a pleasure proper to itself." It is a pleasure, adds Aristotle, that we associate with the gods, of whom it would be "absurd" to think that they "make contracts and return deposits." But as living beings, the gods must do something, and what they do is contemplate.

"Therefore, that which is most akin to this [godly state] must be most of the nature of happiness" (book 10, chapters 7 and 8).

If we put aside the claim of being akin to godliness—made also by St. Thomas Aquinas—this is a perfect account of the academy, a realm where contemplation with no end beyond itself is mandated and "practical activities" are admitted only as the objects of that contemplation. That is the basis of the distinction I have been urging between the kinds of truth sought in the academy—truths sought for their "own sake" independently of any call to action—and the kind of truth sought by those who conduct inquiry with a view to deciding on and implementing policy.

It has been pointed out to me by Hanoch Dagan, professor of law at Tel Aviv University, that some academic disciplines seem committed to both forms of truth seeking. Thus, for example (it is his example), "law by its nature . . . aspires to do justice" and therefore "academic legal work is typically concerned with the justifiability of legal rules, cases, and doctrines" (personal communication). While I agree that law aspires to do justice, I don't think that the academic *study* of law aspires to do justice. Rather it aspires to an accurate account of that aspiration's history and to a measured assessment of the various attempts to realize it. The justifiability that academic legal study focuses on involves an inquiry into the intellectual coherence of rules and doctrines; it does not (or should not) involve a judgment as to whether those rules and doctrines are morally attractive or politically desirable. Such judgments are of course legitimate, but they are the business of legislatures and courts, not of professors in a classroom.

Dagan makes the further argument that advancing knowledge (the job of the academy) and doing justice (the job of the legal system) are similarly situated norms that are "significant in shaping both professions." No, the norms are quite different and that difference is reflected in the professions they shape. Doing justice is a norm that necessarily demands action; advancing knowledge is a norm that stops short of either recommending or taking action. To be sure, contemplation as an end in itself and contemplation as a preliminary to action are both worthy activities. What I have been arguing in this book is that they should not be confused, and that if they are, a certain mode of being—call it academic life or, disparagingly, the Ivory Tower—will have been lost. Maybe it's well lost. Maybe the gain of an academy directly engaged with the world is worth the loss. Maybe the expansion of academic freedom into a concept that flies free of the academy is a good thing. But I don't think so.

Academic Freedom, the First Amendment, and Holocaust Denial (a talk given by the author at Rice University, April 2012)

I

I'm here this evening to talk about the relationship between academic freedom, the First Amendment, and Holocaust denial.

No one of these three is a simple concept, but Holocaust denial is perhaps the most easily characterized. It is what it says, the denial that the Third Reich engaged in a systematic attempt—often called the "final solution"—to eliminate Jews from the face of the earth. Deniers deny that it was Hitler's intention to perform genocide and claim instead that he merely wanted to relocate the Jews; and they also deny that his efforts resulted in the death of six million. Indeed, deniers deny many things—the existence of gas chambers (they were just large dry cleaning machines), the properties of the gas supposedly used in the chambers, the number of Jews who died, the causes of their deaths, the authenticity of Anne Frank's diary. Deniers assert that none of what makes up what they call the Holocaust myth actually happened, and that the "big lie" has been perpetrated by Jews in a successful effort to shame the world into giving them a country, not to mention the millions, perhaps billions, of dollars awarded as reparations. Deniers speak contemptuously of a Holocaust industry, and in response, they themselves have established what amounts to a Holocaust denial industry—complete with websites, books, documentaries, a roster of heroes (some of them credentialed academics), and organizations in almost every country in the world.

Why is Holocaust denial a matter of global concern while round-earth denial, man-on-the-moon denial, and Elvis-is-dead denial are not? The answer is, first, that Holocaust denial is perceived by many as a further assault on the Jews who were the Holocaust's victims, both those who died and those who survived, in addition to the extended victims, those whose relatives entered concentration camps and were never seen again.

A second answer is that Holocaust denial is regarded not only as a crime against persons, but as an epistemological crime—an affront to the reality of history and the sanctity of truth. Holocaust deniers, it is said, do not merely cause harm to the memories of dead people and the psyches of live ones; they undermine the processes by which we establish matters of fact. Holocaust deniers must be answered not only so that a factual matter can be resolved, but so that the very idea of fact can be protected from wholesale subversion.

I believe that this second, metaphysical way of characterizing what Holocaust deniers do is a mistake, both philosophically and tactically. But before I say why, I want to bring in the other two terms of our triad, the First Amendment and academic freedom.

How is the First Amendment related to efforts to combat Holocaust denial? The easy way to answer the question is to survey the manner in which Holocaust denial is regulated in other countries. In France, for example, it is a "violation of law to use the press or any other form of public written communication . . . to deny the existence of crimes against humanity . . . committed by members of a criminal organization as defined by the Nuremberg International Tribunal." In Austria, a person shall be "liable to a penalty . . . if, in print or broadcast or in some other medium, or otherwise publicly in any manner accessible to a large number of people, he denies the National Social genocide" (Article 3h of the Prohibition Act).

In Germany, "Whoever publically, or at a meeting, denies, diminishes, or approves an act committed under the regime of National Socialism . . . shall be punished by imprisonment up to five years" (Article 130 of the Penal Code). In the Czech Republic, the "person who publicly denies, puts in doubt, approves, or tries to justify Nazi or Communist genocide . . . will be punished by prison of six months to three years" (Article 261a of the amended Constitution, 1992). In Luxembourg, it is "forbidden to contest, trivialize, justify or deny publicly the existence of crimes against humanity or war crimes linked to the Holocaust" (Article 457–3 of the revised Criminal Code). These and many more such laws are listed by Michael Whine (2009).

No one of these laws would be held constitutional in the United States; they would all fall under the First Amendment prohibition against abridging the freedom of speech. In order to understand why we must look into the history of the First Amendment, which in the past 115 years has been marked by three stages (there are many substages, but three will do for our purposes this evening).

Stage one—the "bad tendency" theory, in force at the turn of the twentieth century. This says that some forms of speech, whatever their context of utterance, tend to bring about bad effects and therefore do not merit constitutional protection.

Stage two—the "clear and present danger" test. Writing (often in dissent) at the beginning of the twentieth century, Justices Oliver Wendell Holmes and Louis Brandeis argued that the effects of speech could not be determined apart from context, and therefore we should not be quick to criminalize or suppress speech before it has been determined that its feared effects are about to occur. (Neither the left nor the right was happy with the test. The left worried that under it the state would too easily conclude that the danger is clear and imminent. The right worried that the state would delay action until after the damage had already been done.)

Although stages one and two are opposed, they are alike in not according speech an independent status. That is, they are concerned not with speech in and of itself, but with speech as an activity that has effects, and the question they ask (and answer differently) is, What will happen if we allow this kind of speech to flourish?

The effects test was also accompanied by a content test. It was assumed for a long time that some kinds of speech were simply too low-value to deserve constitutional protection. Some of these were listed in a famous paragraph in a 1942 Supreme Court case, *Chaplinsky v. New Hampshire*:

> These include the lewd and obscene, the profane and the libelous, and the insulting or "fighting words"— those which by their very utterance inflict injury or tend to an immediate breach of the peace. It has been well observed that such utterances are no essential part of any exposition of ideas, and are of such slight social value as a step to truth that any benefit derived from them is clearly outweighed by the social interest in order and morality. (*Chaplinsky v. New Hampshire*, 314 U.S. 568)

Almost all of the forms of speech dismissed in this paragraph as being of slight social value or contributing little to the world of ideas have now been brought under the umbrella of First Amendment protection. This is the result of stage three: speech as a value independent of either its effects or its content.

This version of the First Amendment is announced in *New York Times v. Sullivan* (1964), where the Court rejects the traditional view that falsehoods do not merit constitutional protection and announces the trumping value of lively debate. "Debate on public issues should be uninhibited, robust and wide-open." The reasoning is that if the vigor of public discussion is the first priority, falsehoods and defamations do have a place because their utterance will provoke just the kind of discussion you want to encourage. Here is Justice Arthur Goldberg making the point: "Neither factual error nor defamatory content suffices to remove the constitutional shield." Moreover,

Goldberg adds, the right to speak one's mind about public affairs must be upheld "despite the harms which may flow from excesses and abuses" (*New York Times Co. v. Sullivan*, 376 U.S. 254, 273).

These sweeping statements inaugurate a libertarian First Amendment orthodoxy. Speech is not to be sanctioned on the basis either of its content (contribution to truth) or its effects (whether malign or benign), but is to be welcomed into the public square as a contribution to the marketplace of ideas. Anything that is said is presumed to be of value, even blatant misrepresentations and lies. The rule is laid down by the court in *Gertz v. Welch* (1974): "Under the First Amendment, there is no such thing as a false idea" (*Gertz v. Robert Welch, Inc.*, 418 U.S. 323, 339).

We can now see why European-style laws against the profession or publication of denials of the Holocaust will not be permitted under the modern First Amendment dispensation. In the Western democracies surveyed earlier, Holocaust denial is stigmatized and criminalized *because* it is a false idea and therefore no contribution to the search for truth. Holocaust denial is said to be *malum in se*, evil in itself, and the state, it is assumed, has no obligation to allow evil to flourish and every obligation to combat and suppress evil whenever it can in the interest of "order and morality" (*Chaplinsky*). The current form of the First Amendment forbids such a judgment. Ideas may seem to be meretricious and pernicious, but that is merely the verdict of the moment, and history shows that allowing public opinion to set the limits of what can and cannot be said leads to the silencing of dissenting voices and the upholding of a status quo that has not earned its status in the give-and-take of free and open deliberation. Better to allow those voices full expression, and if they prove to be injurious to truth and morality, the workings of the marketplace will expose them as such. Two statements of Justice Brandeis capture the spirit of this view: "Sunshine is said to be the best of disinfectants" ("What Publicity Can Do," *Harper's Weekly*, December 20, 1913), and "The remedy to be applied [for bad speech] is more speech, not enforced silence" (*Whitney v. California,* 274 U.S. 357 [1927]).

II

Here is where we can bring in the third of our master tropes, academic freedom. Academic freedom is a contested concept. There are disagreements about just what it is, who has it, how far its scope extends, whether it is a subset of the First Amendment, whether it is a constitutional right, whether it includes the freedom to pronounce on political matters, whether it insulates the professor from university discipline, and much more. None of these matters will be settled tonight, but amidst the controversy we can identify one uncontroversial basis for the justification of academic freedom in the nature of the job, which is usually characterized as the specifying of the truth about some disputed matter. If you are trying to find out what is true, you must begin by not prejudicing your inquiry. Therefore no point of view should be either anointed or dismissed out of hand in advance. Any and all theses are to be put to the test of rational deliberation, laboratory procedures, the marshaling and assessing of evidence, etc. It follows that the academic researcher must be free to pursue the evidence wherever it leads, even if it leads to a conclusion many abhor, a conclusion like the Holocaust never happened.

In 1915 the fledgling American Association of University Professors issued its Declaration of Principles on Academic Freedom and Academic Tenure. In that seminal and still authoritative document, universities are characterized as "experiment stations" where new ideas may germinate and "where their fruit, although . . . distasteful to the community as a whole, may be allowed to ripen, until finally . . . it may become a part of the accepted intellectual food of the nation." "Distasteful to the community" is a fancy way of saying "unpopular." The idea is that the public's opinion of a viewpoint should not be determinative, or even weighty, in deciding whether it is to be taken seriously as a candidate for truth. Academic conclusions should be reached on the basis of expert knowledge and should not represent "echoes of the opinions of the lay public." As we have seen, exactly the same reasoning informs the oft-repeated commonplace that First Amendment protection should be extended not only to ideas the public affirms, but to ideas the public loathes: "We should be eternally vigilant against attempts to check the expression of opinions that we loathe and believe to be fraught with death" (Oliver Wendell Holmes in *Abrams v. U.S.*, 250 U.S. 616, 630 [1919]).

It is easy to see how the combination of a libertarian First Amendment (expression is to be valued for its own sake) and the doctrine of academic freedom (inquiry should not be blocked by excluding ideas in advance) combine to provide an opening for Holocaust deniers to ply their trade. Rather than placing the emphasis on their specific assertions, deniers can present themselves as the champions of open inquiry and truth—not any particular truth, but truth in general, which, they say, can only be honored as a guiding principle if inquiry is not truncated by refusing even to consider ideas that fly in the face of current wisdom. The home page of Holocaust denier Ernst Zündel's website announces that "the fight for freedom of speech and truth goes on." Not the fight to rehabilitate Hitler's reputation, not the fight to expose the lies of survivors, not the fight to decertify as evidence Anne Frank's diary, but the fight for freedom and truth: We are just doing the work of the Enlightenment, deniers say, and those who would refuse us a venue or censor us or indict us as criminals are not the enemies of Holocaust denial, but the enemies of truth. "The real issues in this matter," Zündel declares, "are not 'anti-Semitism,' 'racism,' or 'hate,' but Truth, Freedom of Speech and Press, Freedom of Enquiry, and ultimately, Justice" (http://www.zundelsite.org/ez-political-bio.html).

It is a brilliant move, one that takes the pressure off the deniers' actual claims and places it instead on the large abstractions at the heart of the liberal state and the Enlightenment project. Liberalism's most cherished convictions and talismanic phrases—freedom of speech, open inquiry, the marketplace of ideas—are invoked by deniers in order to ensure the flourishing of views which, if triumphant, would spell the end of liberalism and, perhaps, of civilization as we know it. The allowing of Holocaust denial, despite its possible deleterious effects, is the realization of another of Holmes's famous pronouncements: "If in the long run the beliefs expressed in . . . dictatorships are destined to be accepted by the dominant forces of the community, the only meaning of free speech is that they should be given their chance and have their way" (*Gitlow v. People of the State of New York*, 268 U.S. 652, 673 [1925]).

One wonders whether Holmes's fatalism was genuine or whether he believed, as Brandeis did, that in the end good speech will drive out the bad, or that, as John Milton put it, truth will always prevail in a "free and open encounter" (Milton 1973). This long-range optimism is offered as the answer to those who fear that in the absence of laws prohibiting it, Holocaust denial cannot be combated. Exactly the reverse, it is argued. If you suppress Holocaust denial, it will flourish underground; its proponents will become martyrs and First Amendment heroes and figures of sympathy. It is better to allow the deniers' arguments full exposure, for in the course of time and the workings of the marketplace of ideas, the weakness of those arguments will become apparent. In short, the antidote is education, coupled, says Michael Whine (2009) "with a wide-spread understanding that denial is a means to undermine or falsify the established facts of history" (556).

III

With this statement Whine enrolls himself in the list of those who charge that Holocaust denial is above all an assault on truth and fact, and you will recall that earlier I called this way of attacking denial a mistake.

Why do I say that? Well, first of all, "defender of truth and fact" is the self-characterization of deniers. It is we, they say, who are for truth and against lies and the distortion of history. But, you might object, the deniers are, in fact, liars; those who oppose them are telling the truth. I trust you can see the weakness of this position, which amounts to name calling. ("Liar, liar, pants on fire.") The next recourse is to say that Holocaust affirmers have evidence—both eyewitness and documentary—while all the deniers have are fabrications, forgeries, and scientific mumbo jumbo, all in the service of a political ideology. Ditto, say the deniers, and we're right back where we started.

Sorting this out must begin with an insight many will resist: Holocaust deniers are not liars, if you mean by liar someone who knows that something is false, but asserts it anyway. My reading of the literature persuades me that deniers, like their opponents, believe what they say, and believe, as affirmers do, that those who don't see what they see are blind or worse.

Nor will it suffice to invoke a distinction between fact and interpretation and declare that while disagreement about how to interpret the Holocaust is inevitable and intellectually healthy, the fact of the Holocaust is undeniable. Here is a statement made to that effect by the Duke University history department: "Historical revision of major events is not concerned with the actuality of these events; rather it concerns their . . . interpretation—their causes and consequences. . . . There is no debate among historians about the actuality of the Holocaust" (statement reprinted in the *Duke Chronicle,* November 13, 1991).

The same point is made by historian Deborah Lipstadt (1993): "the validity of a historical interpretation is determined by how well it accounts for the facts" (25). The commonsense picture here is familiar: the way to settle interpretive disputes is to set the competing interpretations next to the facts and have the facts decide. This is as much to say that at crucial moments, and if given enough space, the facts will speak for themselves and pronounce on which interpretations of them are correct. But if facts were self-declaring, as this fantasy implies they are, there would be very little for historians to do, except, perhaps, for a little tidying up.

In fact (a phrase I do not shrink from), the most vigorous debates about history are not about how to interpret the facts, but about what the facts *are*. The fiction of a baseline level of fact that stands as an obstacle to irresponsible interpretation is just that, a fiction. Everyone claims to be building on a firm substratum of undeniable fact, especially in the political arena where we hear each side proclaim loudly that "while you are entitled to your own interpretation, you are not entitled to your own facts," a tired and clichéd commonplace which assumes that facts are identifiable apart from any interpretation of them. They are not. Rather than preceding interpretation, facts are established in the course of interpretation. When they are established (at least to the satisfaction of responsible observers), facts will be received as plain and inescapable, but because their plainness is the product of interpretive struggle, it is always vulnerable to a new round of interpretive dispute at the end of which a new plainness (and with it new facts) will have emerged. That process—theoretically interminable—is what Holocaust deniers are engaged in, and while many dismiss their claims as being beyond the pale of rational inquiry, they are no less rational than their opponents. Rationality can be the property of those who are in the wrong as well as of those who are in the right.

So you can't stop Holocaust denial by pointing to the facts as if they were freestanding or by waving the banner of reason, any more than you can stop Holocaust denial by labeling yourself a truth-speaker and your opponents liars. These gestures may be satisfying to perform, but they don't do the job.

IV

How then do you stop it?

If by that question you mean how do you stop it from circulating in the culture of the United States, there is no satisfactory answer. As we have seen, under a libertarian First Amendment, the circulation of Holocaust denial is constitutionally protected and laws suppressing it will never succeed in the courts. And as for education, the remedy promoted by Michael Whine and others, educating is what all sides in these controversies claim to be doing, and, given the nature of the internet, it is even more difficult than usual to tell the difference between education and propaganda, although you can be sure that every party will claim to be on the right side of that line.

Some think that Holocaust denial will be stopped by the functioning of the "marketplace of ideas." That metaphor promises that if we allow all voices to be heard, in time the voices speaking truth will triumph over the voices speaking falsehoods, and Holocaust denial will be vanquished. Holocaust denial will, in effect, stop itself. But this reverse Gresham's law has little support in history and flies in the face of what we see every day, especially now that Citizens United is the law of the land. Put Holocaust denial into the mix of ideas available to the public, and it will flourish, not wither in the light of day.

All, however, is not lost. If you mean by the question how do you stop it?, how can it be kept out of the classroom?, and how can deniers be prevented from gaining positions in university history departments?, the answer is that it has already been stopped, and the mechanism by which this has been accomplished is on display in the last sentence of the Duke history department's statement cited above: "There is no debate among historians about the actuality of the Holocaust."

Actually, there is debate among historians. David Irving is a historian, Harry Elmer Barnes and David Leslie Hoggan were historians, and there are others with academic credentials who have trafficked in Holocaust denial. But they all have either been professionally discredited or dismissed from their posts or exiled from the academy or indicted as criminals. So that when the Duke history department looks around in the discipline and finds no debate about the actuality of the Holocaust, it is because the discipline has made certain that there shall be none. No historian who thinks the Holocaust didn't happen will be hired by this department or by any other. This was made absolutely clear by the American Historical Association when in 1991 it declared in a formal statement that "No serious historian questions that the Holocaust took place." This is so only because "serious historian" has been defined by the gatekeepers of the discipline as someone who affirms the Holocaust. The Association is offering as an independent observation the existence of a state of affairs it has decreed.

This is obviously a circular procedure and an exercise of power to boot, but it can, nevertheless, be justified. When the Duke history department and the AHA exclude Holocaust deniers from their ranks—not as a matter of law or morality, but as a matter of professional judgment—they are not doing so in a cavalier or capricious manner. Rather, they are standing on a thick record of research by men and women with impeccable credentials and publications that have been vetted by the most exacting standards. This is not an arbitrary act of exclusion, but an act of exclusion that issues from the collective expertise of an entire discipline or guild. Now of course the wisdom of the guild is not infallible and could in time be overturned by a new wisdom. But until that happens, received academic wisdom occupies a privileged position, and the obstacles to dislodging it are rightly very high because the privileged position has been earned. The proposer of a counterintuitive thesis like the Holocaust didn't happen must earn his entry into the discussion. He cannot claim it simply because he has a viewpoint and wants it to be heard.

Here we see a difference between the First Amendment and academic freedom. The First Amendment stands for the proposition that all points of view must be given a hearing and none excluded; and while academic freedom also insists that ideas should be given a hearing, it erects a barrier that must be negotiated before a particular idea is welcomed into the conversation as a legitimate participant; it must pass muster before a body of credentialed experts; and if it does not, it will be sent away without apology and without any philosophical or moral anxieties. The academy is not a democracy; it is a structure of authority, and it is in the business of excluding what it has judged to be unworthy. And at least for the foreseeable future, Holocaust denial is not going to get through the door.

V

At this point, a sincere Holocaust denier—and we must assume that there are such—will protest and ask, "Isn't the determination of the truth what the academy is all about?" Yes, it is, but the academy's method of determining the truth is cumulative and collaborative, a matter of marshaling and weighing evidence that, when validated, provides the basis on which research henceforth proceeds. There is then a bias, but an innocent one, in favor of the conclusions that have been reached in the long course of scholarly investigation and deliberation. When "truth" is invoked by the Holocaust denier or the possessor of any other outlier thesis—like the thesis that Shakespeare did not write Shakespeare's plays—the appeal is to a truth that supposedly transcends all disciplinary pronouncements. True is what is true, not what the guild says is true, the denier will insist. But in the academic world—as opposed to the world of democracy—what is true *is* what the guild says is true, for after all, as Thomas Kuhn (1996) declares in *The Structure of Scientific Revolutions*, "There is no standard higher than the assent of the relevant community" (94).

Of course there *is* ultimately a higher standard—a standard of truth as seen from a God's-eye point of view. That view, however, is not ours. We still see through a glass darkly, and so we must put our trust, however provisionally, in that glass or perspective that at least for now bears the preponderance of authority. The exclusion of Holocaust deniers from the academy is the work not of Truth with a capital *T*, but of an authorized expertise. Authorized by whom? By the community of experts. Again, this is circular, but it works. That is why the Duke history department and the American Historical Association are able to look around and say with perfect confidence, "No Holocaust deniers here!" There is, alas, no comparable mechanism of exclusion in the American culture at large; which means that like Creation Science, birtherism, 9/11 truthism, and black helicopters sent at the direction of Queen Elizabeth, Holocaust denial is here to stay.

WORKS CITED

Abbott, Andrew. 1988. *The System of Professions: An Essay on the Division of Expert Labor.* Chicago: University of Chicago Press.

Alexander, Larry. 2006. "Academic Freedom." *University of Colorado Law Review* 77.

American Association of University Professors. 1915. "Declaration of Principles on Academic Freedom and Academic Tenure." www .aaup.org/report/1915-declaration-principles-academic-freedom -and-academic-tenure.

———. 2006. "On Academic Boycotts." www.aaup.org/report/aca demic-boycotts.

Areen, Judith. 2009. "Government as Educator: A New Understanding of First Amendment Protection of Academic Freedom and Governance." *Georgetown Law Journal* 97.

Barendt, Eric. 2010. *Academic Freedom and the Law: A Comparative Study.* Oxford: Hart.

Barghouti, Omar. 2011. *Boycott, Divestment, Sanctions: The Global Struggle for Palestinian Rights.* Chicago: Haymarket.

BRICUP. 2007. *Why Boycott Israeli Universities?* London: BRICUP.

Butler, Judith. 2003. "No, It's Not Anti-Semitic." *London Review of Books* (August 21).

———. 2006a. "Academic Norms, Contemporary Challenges: A Reply to Robert Post on Academic Freedom." In *Academic Freedom after September 11*, ed. Beshara Doumani. New York: Zone Books.

———. 2006b. "Israel/Palestine and the Paradoxes of Academic Freedom." *Radical Philosophy* 135.

———. 2009. "Critique, Dissent, Disciplinarity." *Critical Inquiry* 35.

Byrne, J. Peter. 1989. "Academic Freedom: A 'Special Concern of the First Amendment.'" *Yale Law Journal* 99.

———. 2004. "The Threat to Constitutional Academic Freedom." *Journal of College and University Law* 31.

———. 2006. "Constitutional Academic Freedom after *Grutter:* Getting Real about the 'Four Freedoms' of a University." *University of Colorado Law Review* 77.

Clark, Burton R. 1971. "Faculty Organization and Authority." In *Academic Governance: Research on Institutional Policy and Decision Making*, ed. J. Victor Baldridge. Richmond, CA: McCutchan.

DelFattore, Joan. 2011. "Defending Academic Freedom in the Age of *Garcetti.*" *Academe* 97.1.

Downing, David B. 2005. "The Knowledge Contract: Politics and Paradigms in the Academic Workplace." Lincoln: University of Nebraska Press.

Duderstadt, James. 2004. "Governing the Twenty-First Century University." In *Competing Conceptions of Academic Governance: Negotiating the Perfect Storm,* ed. William G. Tierney. Baltimore, MD: Johns Hopkins University Press.

Farley, Lara Geer. 2007. "A Matter of Public Concern: 'Official Duties' of Employment Gag Public Employee Free Speech Rights." *Washburn Law Journal* 46.

Farred, Grant. 2008–2009. "The Act of Politics Is to Divide." *Works and Days* 26–27.

Finkin, Matthew. 1988. "Intramural Speech, Academic Freedom, and the First Amendment." *Texas Law Review* 66.

Finkin, Matthew W., and Robert C. Post. 2009. *For the Common Good: Principles of American Academic Freedom.* New Haven, CT: Yale University Press.

Forte, Maximilian. 2009. "Canadian Academic Boycott of Israel: Why We Need to Take Action." On Zero Anthropology blog, February 4. http://zeroanthropology.net/2009/02/04/canadian-academic-boy cott-of-israel-why-we-need-to-take-action/.

Freeston, Jesse. 2009. "Dismissing Critical Pedagogy: Denis Rancourt vs. University of Ottawa." At rabble.ca., January 12. http://rabble .ca/news/dismissing-critical-pedagogy-denis-rancourt-vs-univer sity-ottawa.

Freidson, Eliot. 1970. *Profession of Medicine: A Study of the Sociology of Applied Knowledge.* New York: Dodd, Mead.

Fuller, Steve. 2000. *Thomas Kuhn: A Philosophical History for Our Time.* Chicago: University of Chicago Press.

Gajda, Amy. 2009. *The Trials of Academe: The New Era of Campus Litigation.* Cambridge, Mass.: Harvard University Press.

Gerber, Larry. 2001. "'Inextricably Linked': Shared Governance and Academic Freedom." *Academe* 87.3.

———. 2010. "Professionalization as the Basis for Academic Freedom and Faculty Governance." *Journal of Academic Freedom* 1.

Giroux, Henry. 2008. *Against the Terror of Neoliberalism: Politics beyond the Age of Greed.* Boulder, CO: Paradigm.

———. 2010. "Academic Unfreedom in America." In *Academic*

Freedom in the Post-9/11 Era, ed. Edward J. Carvalho and David B. Downing. New York: Palgrave Macmillan.

Goldberg, Erica, and Kelly Sarabyn. 2011. "Measuring a 'Degree of Deference': Institutional Academic Freedom in a Post-*Grutter* World." *Santa Clara Law Review* 51.1.

Haskell, Thomas. 1996. "Justifying the Rights of Academic Freedom." In *The Future of Academic Freedom,* ed. Louis Menand. Chicago: University of Chicago Press.

Hofstadter, Richard, and Walter Metzger. 1955. *The Development of Academic Freedom in the United States.* New York: Columbia University Press.

Horwitz, Paul. 2007. "Universities as First Amendment Institutions." *UCLA Law Review* 54.

Kant, Immanuel. 1784. "What Is Enlightenment?" In *The Art of Theory, Conversations in Political Philosophy.* www.artoftheory .com/what-is-enlightenment_immanuel-kant/.

———. 1798. *The Conflict of Faculties,* trans. and intro. Mary J. Gregor. Lincoln: University of Nebraska Press, 1992.

Karran, Terrence. 2009. "Academic Freedom: In Justification of a Universal Ideal." *Studies in Higher Education* 34, no. 2.

Keller, George. 2004. "Traditional Governance in US Education." In *Competing Conceptions of Academic Governance: Negotiating the Perfect Storm,* ed. William G. Tierney. Baltimore, MD: Johns Hopkins University Press.

King, Stacey. 2002. "Who Owns Academic Freedom ?: The Standard For Academic Free Speech at Public Universities." *Washington and Lee Law Review* 59 (Winter).

Klein, Daniel B., and Andrew Western. 2005. "Equal Representation Is a Tenet of Democracy, Yet Academic Republicans Are Being Eradicated by Academic Democrats." *Palo Alto Weekly,* online ed., February 23.

Kuhn, Thomas. 1996. *The Structure of Scientific Revolutions,* 3rd ed. Chicago: University of Chicago Press.

Landry, Alison Paige. 2001. "Professorial Speech and Academic Freedom: Implications of the Fourth Circuit's Decision in *Urofsky v. Gilmore.*" Paper presented at the Twenty-Second Annual National Conference on Law and Higher Education, Stetson University College of Law, Tampa, FL.

Larson, Magali. 1977. *The Rise of Professionalism: A Sociological Analysis.* Berkeley: University of California Press.

Lipstadt, Deborah E. 1993. *Denying the Holocaust: The Growing Assault on Truth and Memory*. New York: Free Press.

Lovejoy, Arthur O. 1930. "Academic Freedom." In *The Encyclopedia of Social Sciences*. New York: Macmillan.

Lukanioff, Greg. 2012. *Unlearning Liberty: Campus Censorship and the End of American Debate*. New York: Encounter.

MacIntyre, Alasdair. 1981. *After Virtue: A Study in Moral Theory*. Notre Dame, IN: University of Notre Dame Press.

McClennen, Sophia A. 2010. "The Crisis of Intellectual Engagement." In *Academic Freedom in the Post-9/11 Era*, ed. Edward J. Carvalho and David B. Downing. New York: Palgrave Macmillan.

Milton, John, 1973. *Areopagitica and Of Education*, ed. K. M. Lea. Oxford: Clarendon.

Moodie, Graeme C. 1996. "On Justifying the Different Claims to Academic Freedom." *Minerva* 34.

Nelson, Cary. 2010. *No University Is an Island: Saving Academic Freedom*. New York: New York University Press.

Nussbaum, Martha. 2007. "Against Academic Boycotts." *Dissent* 54.3.

O'Neil, Robert. 2008. "Academic Speech in the Post-*Garcetti* Environment." *First Amendment Law Review* 7.

———. 2009. "Academic Freedom in Cyberspace." *Academe* 95.5. http://www.aaup.org/article/academic-freedom-cyberspace#.Ujtm8BZD5SU.

Palestinian Campaign for the Academic and Cultural Boycott of Israel. "Guidelines for Applying the International Academic Boycott of Israel. October 1. http://www.pacbi.org/etemplate.php?id=1107.

Post, Robert. 2006. "The Structure of Academic Freedom." In *Academic Freedom after September 11*, ed. Beshara Doumani. New York: Zone Books.

———. 2009. "Debating Disciplinarity." *Critical Inquiry* 35.

———. 2012. *Democracy, Expertise, and Academic Freedom: A First Amendment Jurisprudence for the Modern State*. New Haven, CT: Yale University Press.

Rabban, David. 1990. "A Functional Analysis of 'Individual' and 'Institutional' Academic Freedom under the First Amendment." *Law and Contemporary Problems* 53.

———. 1998. "Can Academic Freedom Survive Postmodernism?" *California Law Review* 86.

Radhakrishnan, R. 2008–2009. "Is Freedom Academic?" *Works and Days* 26–27.

Rancourt, Denis. 2007. "Academic Squatting: A Democratic Method of Curriculum Development." *Our Schools, Our Selves* 16.3.

Redden, Elizabeth. 2013. "Backing the Israel Boycott." *Inside Higher Education*. www.insidehighered.com/news/2013/12.17/american -studies-association-backs-boycott-israeli-universities

Raz, Joseph. 2009. *Between Authority and Interpretation: On the Theory of Law and Practical Reason.* Oxford: Oxford University Press.

Rendleman, Doug. 2002. "Academic Freedom in *Urofsky*'s Wake." *Washington and Lee Law Review* 59 (Winter).

Robinson, William I. 2009. Speech at the Seventh Annual International Al-Awda Convention, Garden Grove, CA, May 23.

Rorty, Richard. 1996. "Does Academic Freedom Have Philosophical Presuppositions?" In *The Future of Academic Freedom,* ed. Louis Menand. Chicago: University of Chicago Press.

Rosenthal, Lawrence. 1998. "Permissible Content Discrimination under the First Amendment: The Strange Case of the Public Employee." *Hastings Constitutional Law Quarterly* 25.

Said, Edward. 1994. *Representations of the Intellectual.* New York: Pantheon.

Schauer, Frederick. 2006. "Is There a Right to Academic Freedom?" *University of Colorado Law Review* 77.

Schmidt, Peter. 2011. "AAUP Report Denounces Suspension of Idaho State U. Faculty Senate." *The Chronicle of Higher Education* online, May 26.

Scott, Joan. 1996. "Academic Freedom as an Ethical Practice." In *The Future of Academic Freedom,* ed. Louis Menand. Chicago: University of Chicago Press.

Searle, John. 1997. "Rationality and Realism, What Is at Stake." In *Academic Freedom and Tenure: Ethical Issues,* ed. Richard T. DeGeorge. Lanham, MD: Roman and Littlefield.

Tepper, Robert J., and Craig G. White. 2009. "Speak No Evil: Academic Freedom and the Application of *Garcetti v. Ceballos* to Public University Faculty." *Catholic University Law Review* 59.

Thomson, Judith Jarvis. 1990. "Ideology and Faculty Selection." *Law and Contemporary Problems* 53.

Van Alstyne, William W. 1990. "Academic Freedom and the First Amendment in the Supreme Court of the United States: An Unhurried Historical Review." *Law and Contemporary Problems* 53.3.

———. 2009. Comment on O'Neil (2009).

Weaver, Russell L., Catherine Hancock, Donald E. Lively, and John C. Knechtle. 2011. *The First Amendment: Cases, Problems, Materials.* New York: NexisLexis.

Weber, Max. 1918. "Science as a Vocation." Speech at Munich University. http://mail.www.anthropos-lab.net/wp/wp-content /uploads/2011/12/Weber-Science-as-a-Vocation.pdf.

Weinrib, Ernest. 1988. "Legal Formalism: On the Immanent Rationality of Law." *Yale Law Journal* 97.6.

Whine, Michael. 2009. "Expanding Holocaust Denial and Legislation against It." *In Extreme Speech and Democracy,* ed. Ivan Hare and James Weinstein. New York: Oxford University Press.

Yudof, Mark. 1988. "Intramural Musings on Academic Freedom: A Reply to Professor Finkin." *Texas Law Review* 66.

INDEX

Abbott, Andrew, 33

Abrams v. U.S. (1919), 143

Academic Bill of Rights, 71

academic culture: as conservative, 66; and higher education, 129–31

academic freedom, 4–5, 19, 130, 131–32, 135

—academic abstention, 101–3

—academic exceptionalism, ix; and professionalism, 104; rejection of, 75, 81

—academic exceptionalism school, 11–12, 16, 74–75, 77, 86, 95–96, 99, 103; and Israeli boycott, 122–23

—academic freedom as critique school, 12–13

—academic freedom as revolution school, 13–14, 51

—academic profession, as peculiar to, 5–6

—authority, as structure of, 148

—and balance, 35–36

—for the common good school, 10–13, 37, 44, 69, 118–19, 122; and indirect effect, 119–20; and Israeli boycott, 118–22

—as contested concept, 142

—and courts, 101–3

—and critical inquiry, 92, 97

—and critique school, 68, 71, 86, 108, 125–26; and Israeli boycott, 123–24

—definitions of, 6

—and democracy, 44–49, 129

—dissent, protection for, 13

—employer's control over, 1–2

—and First Amendment, 9–10, 51–52, 77, 81, 98, 137–38, 142–43, 148

—form and content, distinction between, 82, 85, 89

—as general obligation, 82

—as general value, 5–6

—government-as-employer and government-as-educator, distinction between, 91

—and Holocaust denial, 137, 147, 149

—human freedom, trumping of, 112–13

—institution and teacher, as special, tension between, 51

—intellectual diversity, 71–72

——intramural criticism, 92–97

—Israeli-Palestinian question, 67–68

—Israeli universities, boycott of, 109–17

—it's just a job school, 9–12, 16–17, 20, 24, 30, 36, 38, 40–41, 43–44, 49, 69, 118, 132; academicizing of, 31–32; and Israeli boycott, 118; and neutrality, 34

—justification of, ix, 1, 24–25, 48–49

—as legal concept, viii–ix, 86

—opposing views of, 6

—as limited, guild concept, 82

—new fields, and burden of proof, 64–65

—and pedagogical approach, 53

academic freedom (*continued*)
—political freedom, debate over, 110–17
—and politics, 7, 29–30, 35–36, 133
—and practices, 22–24
—as professional concept, viii–ix, 3, 52–54, 115, 117, 126–27
—and professionalism, 20–22, 27, 73, 104–8
—and professorial speech, 85–87, 90–91, 96–98; and public concern, 83
—professor versus institution, debate over, 109
—as revolution, 124
—schools of, 1, 7, 9–14
—and shared governance, 37–40, 42–44, 47
—and truth, 26–28, 132–34, 142, 149
—as universal ideal, 1, 3
—and virtue, 63, 103
"Academic Freedom" (Karran), 1, 4
Academic Freedom and the Law (Barendt), vii
Academic Freedom Studies, 7
academic politics, 30
academics: as cultural saviors, 48; and elitism, 47; special freedoms of, 5
activity freedom, 5, 52
"Against Academic Boycotts" (Nussbaum), 120
Alexander, Larry, 19
American Association of University Professors (AAUP), 16, 39, 122; Declaration of Principles on Academic Freedom and Academic

Tenure (1915), 2–3, 10–12, 21, 38, 45, 47, 50, 54, 75, 95–96, 132, 142; and elitism, 47; and employment-at-will, 96; and Israeli universities boycott, 118–20
American Historical Association (AHA), 147–49
American studies, 128
American Studies Association (ASA), 127–28
Americans with Disabilities Act, 100
antifoundationalism, 55
Aquinas, Thomas, 134
Areen, Judith, 91, 97
Aristotle, 133
Arizona, 127
Association for Asian American Studies, 127
Atlas Shrugged (Rand), 9
Austria, 138

Bailey, John Michael, 8
Baker, Mona, 113–14
Barendt, Eric, vii
Barghouti, Omar, 112
Barnes, Harry Elmer, 147
BB&T, 9
Bergan, S., 4
Board of Curators v. Horowitz (1978), 101
Boyer, J. W., 4
Brandeis, Louis, 139, 141, 144
Branzburg v. Hayes (1972), 98–99
Bush, George W., 62, 121
Butler, Judith, 13, 15, 51, 53, 62–63, 69, 71, 73–74, 108, 114–17, 125–26, 133; on academic work and

academic life, 57–58; and critique, 61, 66–68, 70; on education and indoctrination, 55; on Israeli-Palestinian question, 67–68; norms, as historically challengeable, 59–60; Post, debates with, 54–55, 57, 59; professional norms, challenging of, 64; professional norms, and historical conventions, 54; and public interest, 61; rogue viewpoint of, 67, 70

Byrne, J. Peter, viii, 6, 28, 45, 48–49, 87, 101, 129–31

Capone, Al, 122
Ceballos, Richard, 87–89
Chaplinsky v. New Hampshire (1942), 140–41
Citizens United v. Federal Election Commission (2010), 147
Clash of Civilizations and the Remaking of World Order (Huntington), 32–33
Clark, Burton R., 50–51
Concordia University, 111
Connick v. Myers, 78–81, 88, 91, 95, 103
contemplation, 133–35
critical pedagogy, 123
Czech Republic, 139

Dagan, Hanoch, 134
deconstruction, 55
Delaware State College, 92
DelFattore, Joan, 94
Demers v. Austin (2013), 83
democracy, 11; and academic freedom, 44–49, 129;

academic values, tension between, 37; and expertise, 45
Democracy, Expertise, and Academic Freedom (Post), 44–45
Derrida, Jacques, 57, 66
DiMeglio v. Haines (1995), 85
Downing, David, 66
Duderstadt, James, 42–43
Duke University, 145, 147–49

Edley, Christopher, Jr., 62
education, 20; and political action, 14
Education Act (New Zealand) (1989), viii
Education Reform Act (United Kingdom) (1968), viii
Eisenhower, Dwight, 39
elitism, 47–48
End of History and the Last Man, The (Fukuyama), 32
England, 127. *See also* United Kingdom
Enlightenment, 143
Equal Employment Opportunity Commission (EEOC), 100
Equal Protection Clause, 100–101

Farley, Lara Geer, 88
Farred, Grant, 14, 124
Finkin, Matthew, 74, 83, 94–95, 97
First Amendment, 12, 47, 56, 80, 86, 91; and academic freedom, 9–10, 51–52, 98, 137–38, 142–43, 148; "bad tendency" theory, 139; citizen and employee speech, distinction between, 88–90; "clear and present danger"

Israel, 70–71; and Butler, 67–68; Israeli universities, boycott of, 109–20, 127–28; Robinson e-mail, criticism of, 8–9, 15, 17–19

Jolicoeur, Marc, 104, 107

Kant, Immanuel, 42, 97, 125–26; and reason, 41
Karran, Terrence, 1, 3–4
Keller, George, 43–44
Kennedy, Anthony, 87–89
King, Martin Luther, Jr., 8, 15, 17–18, 32
Kissinger, Henry, 122
Klein, Daniel B., 72
Kuhn, Thomas, 60, 63, 149
Kushner, Tony, 8

Landry, Alison Paige, 86
Larson, Magali, 21
law, 23, 134
liberalism, 143–44
Lipstadt, Deborah, 145
literary criticism, 27
literary studies, 33, 59; theory revolution in, 60
Lovejoy, Arthur O., 2
Lukanioff, Greg, 32
Luttig, J. Michael, 81
Luxembourg, 139

MacIntyre, Alasdair, 63
Manan, Wan, 4
Marshall, Thurgood, 78
McClennen, Sophia A., 123
Metzger, Walter, 96
Milton, John, 144
Modern Language Association (MLA), 127

Moodie, Graeme C., 4–5, 40, 52
Moore, Michael, 61
Murnaghan, Francis D., 83–84
Myers, Sheila, 79–80

Nazis, 15, 120
Nelson, Cary, 16
New York Times v. Sullivan (1964), 140–41
New York University (NYU), 40
New Zealand, viii
Nicomachean Ethics (Aristotle), 133
N.L.R.B. v. Yeshiva University (1980), 43
Nuremberg International Tribunal, 138
Nussbaum, Martha, 120; failure to reward, 121–22

Occupy movement, 127
O'Neil, Robert, 90
Oxford University, 121–22

Palestinian Campaign for the Academic and Cultural Boycott of Israel, 110
Perich, Cheryl, 100
Picher, Michel, 109
Pickering v. Board of Education (1968), 78–81, 88, 91, 95, 103
Pilgrim's Progress, The (Bunyan), 99
positivism, 132
postmodernism, 55
Post, Robert, 44, 46–47, 49, 51–53, 55, 59, 63, 74, 129; and democratic competence, 45; education and indoctrination, distinction between on, 54; and professional norms, 54, 57

University of Michigan Law School, 100
University of Ottawa, 108
University of Virginia, 21
Urofsky v. Gilmore (2000), 12, 75–77, 80–87, 95

Van Alstyne, William, 19, 32
Vietnam War, 119
Virginia, 9, 12, 75–76
Virginia Freedom of Information Act, 76

Weber, Max, 31–32, 35, 128
Weinrib, Ernest, 21, 24–25, 61; and immanent intelligibility, 22; and tort law, 23
Western, Andrew, 72

"What Is Enlightenment?" (Kant), 41, 97
Whine, Michael, 139, 144, 146
White, Byron, 78–79
White, Craig G., 91, 97
Whitney v. California (1927), 141–42
Wieman v. Updegraff (1952), 46
Wilkins, William, 76–77, 80, 86
Wilkinson, J. Harvie, III, 81–84
women's studies, 58–59

Yoo, John, 62–63
Yudof, Mark, 5–6, 94, 97

Zündel, Ernst, 143
Zionism, 32